EP Math 2

Parent's Guide

Welcome to the EP Math 2 Parent's Guide!

This little book was created to help you go offline while following EP's Math 2 curriculum. You will need the Math 2 student workbook for your child. Without the online lessons, you will need to be your child's teacher. The directions are here for introducing new topics. The workbook will provide practice and review.

This book also includes objectives for each day, materials marked where needed, directions for what to do each day, and the complete answer key.

There are many days when the students are told to color something, so crayons are listed as a material needed. Where I marked them as optional, there is just something on the page to color for fun, and they aren't needed to complete the lesson.

They will be learning the rest of the addition and subtraction facts this year. You might want to have a place where you hang up the "fact of the day" and recruit family members to randomly quiz your child on it.

And a little note: To avoid calling all children "he" or the awkward phrasing of "him or her," I've used the plural pronoun when referring to your child, such as, "Show the clock to your child and have <u>them</u> point to the hour hand."

Have a great year.

Lee

Review

Day 1 (brown crayon)

- Students will: practice addition facts up to 5 + 4, count the value of coins
- Day 1 worksheet
- We'll be learning the new facts above 5 this year. However, they can be working on their addition and subtraction facts through 9 + 9 and 18 − 9. Use games, flash cards, our facts practice books, etc.

Day 2 (crayons)

- Students will: practice subtraction facts through 10 − 5, create a bar graph with counting and coloring
- Day 2 worksheet
  - Your child will probably need more direction for the bar graph portion of the page. The first letter at the bottom is an A. They will count up the As in Say Easy Peasy! and color in that many blocks above the letter A.
    - There are three As, so they would color in three blocks above the A.
  - Then they will do that with each letter and the exclamation point.
  - It's nice to use a different color for each. They could even color in the letter to match the graph they made, but it could be done all one color.

Day 3

- Students will: practice adding with multiple addends, identify fractions from a representative picture
- Review fractions briefly with your child.
  - Have your child draw a circle and then divide it in half.
  - Ask your child to color in one half of it.
  - Ask how many parts of the circle are there and how many are colored in.
    - There are two parts and one is colored in.
    - Show your child how to write ½ with numbers. That means there are two parts, but one is colored.
  - Ask your child to draw a line across the middle of the circle to divide it into four parts.
  - Ask your child how many parts there are and how many are colored in.
    - There are four parts and two are colored in.
    - Ask your child what that would look like as a fraction.
      - What number would be on the bottom? That's the number of parts.
        - 4
      - What number would be on the top? That's the number colored in.
        - 2
- Day 3 worksheet

Day 4

- Students will: practice subtraction facts up to 9 - 5, read analog clocks to the half hour
- Review reading a clock with your child.
    - Use the clock below. Draw on the time three o'clock. See if your child can read the time.
    - Remind your child that the shorter hand is the one pointing to the hour. The longer hand is the minute hand and it travels around one time every hour.
    - Draw your finger around the clock showing where the minute hand travels over an hour. Have your child do the same.
    - Ask your child how far would the minute hand travel over half an hour. If it had gone just halfway around, where would it be?
    - Halfway around the clock is 30 minutes. This clock says 3 o'clock. In half an hour it would be 3:30.
    - Show your child the next clock. Ask your child to show you the hour hand and the minute hand.
        - What number is the hour hand after?
            - 6, It hasn't gotten to 7 o'clock yet. It's traveled halfway there so far.
        - Where is the minute hand?
            - It's halfway around. It's been thirty minutes since it was six o'clock.
        - Ask your child what time it says.
            - 6:30
- Day 4 worksheet

Day 5 (crayons)
- Students will: practice addition and subtraction facts, develop memory skills
- Day 5 worksheet
- Play a memory game. "I went to a party and I met Amanda." The next person says the same thing but adds on a girl's name that starts with the letter B. Continue on through the alphabet.

Counting/Skip Counting

Day 6 (crayons)
- Students will: count on, recognize patterns, skip count by tens between 200 and 300
- Give your child this thinking quiz.
  - How many numbers past fifty is fifty-three?
    - three
  - How many numbers past forty is forty-four?
    - four
  - How many numbers past fifty-five is fifty-seven?
    - two
  - How many numbers past sixty-five is sixty-eight?
    - three
  - How many numbers past one hundred ten is one hundred fourteen?
    - four
- Day 6 worksheet
  - They are going to skip a page to get there. They will color in the 1s column, all the numbers that end in one.
- Day 6+ worksheet
  - They will fill in the first column, all the numbers ending in 1. The first is 201.
- Make sure your child is keeping up with facts learning.

Day 7 (crayons)
- Students will: count by twos, recognize patterns, count by tens between 200 and 300
- Have your child open to the Day 6 worksheet. Have your child put their finger on the two and skip count by twos. Two, four, six,... as long as you like.
- Now ask your child to continue counting where you stop.
  - Count, "Two, four, six, eight." Ask your child what number would come next in the pattern.
  - Now try: thirty, thirty-two, thirty-four,... What comes next?
- Continued...

- Day 7 worksheet
  - If they get stuck on filling in a blank, remind them to use the Day 6 page to skip count.
- Day 6+ worksheet
  - Fill in the twos column with all the numbers that end in two. These will all be one more than what was filled in on Day 6.

Day 8
- Students will: skip count by threes, recognize patterns, count by tens between 200 and 300
- Day 8 worksheet
  - They can use the connect-the-dots to help them with the second portion of the worksheet if necessary.
- Day 6+ worksheet
  - Fill in the threes column with all the numbers that end in three.
- Don't forget to be working on math facts.

Day 9 (crayons)
- Students will: skip count by fives, recognize patterns, count by tens between 200 and 300
- Day 9 worksheet
- Play with your child, What Comes Next?
  - When counting by fives, what number would come after ten?
    - 15
  - What would come after twenty?
    - 25
  - What would come after thirty-five?
    - 40
  - Have your child ask you.

Day 10
- Students will: count on, count by tens, recognize patterns, count by tens between 200 and 300
- Do this little activity with your child.
  - Ask your child how many more from thirty-two is thirty-five?
    - three
  - Ask your child how many more from twenty-six is twenty-nine?
    - three
  - Ask your child how many more from forty-three is forty-eight?
    - five
- Day 10 worksheet
- Day 6+ worksheet
  - Fill in the tens column, the last one. Every number should end in a zero.

Addition Facts/Comparing Numbers

Day 11
- Students will: practice known subtraction facts, learn the math fact $2 + 6 = 8$
- Learn $2 + 6 = 8$ and $6 + 2 = 8$
  - Have your child say it out loud: six plus two equals eight, two plus six equals eight. $6 + 2 = 8$, $2 + 6 = 8$
  - What does six plus two equal? Clap the answer.
    - Clap eight times because two plus six equals eight.
- Day 11+ worksheet
  - Have your child write the fact both ways on the first 11+ worksheet.
- Day 11 worksheet

Day 12
- Students will: learn the math fact $6 + 3 = 9$
- Teach your child six plus three equals nine, and three plus six equals nine.
  - Have your child say them out loud.
    - $6 + 3 = 9$, $3 + 6 = 9$
  - Ask your child, "What does six plus three equal?"
    - Have your child jump the answer.
      - Jump up and down nine times because six plus three equals nine.
- Day 11+ worksheet
  - Have your child fill in this fact both ways on the first 11+ worksheet.
- Day 12 worksheet

Day 13
- Students will: practice known subtraction facts, learn the math fact $6 + 4 = 10$
- Teach your child $6 + 4 = 10$.
  - Ask your child what $4 + 6$ equals.
    - It equals ten because it doesn't matter which way you add.
      - If you had three coins in your left hand and five coins in your right hand, how many coins would you have?
        - 8 coins
      - How many would you have if you switched hands?
        - You'd still have 8 coins. It doesn't matter which number comes first when you add. You are just putting them all together.
    - Tell your child that four plus six equals ten. Ask your child to stomp the answer to six plus four.
      - Stomp ten times because six plus four equals ten.
- Day 11+ worksheet
  - Have your child write this fact both ways on the first 11+ facts worksheet.
- Day 13 worksheet

Day 14
- Students will: compare numbers up to 100, use the greater than/less than symbol, count to 500 by tens
- Review the greater than/less than symbol with your child.
    - Ask your child which number is bigger 45 or 51.
        - The answer is 51.
    - Write the numbers and draw the greater than symbol between them.
        - 45 < 51
    - Have your child point to the little end of the symbol, the pointy end. Is it pointing to the smaller number?
        - yes
    - Have your child point to the big open end of the symbol. Is it on the side of the bigger number?
        - yes
    - Have your child choose two numbers and write them down.
        - Have your child say which is biggest and what the symbol should look like between them.
        - Have your child draw the symbol.
- Day 14 worksheet

Day 15
- Students will: practice known addition facts, compare numbers up to 1000
- Have your child read the numbers out loud to practice reading larger numbers.
- Day 15 worksheet

Day 16
- Students will: practice known subtraction facts, count even numbers by two, learn the math fact 6 + 5 = 11
- Teach your child 6 + 5 = 11 and 5 + 6 = 11.
    - Have your child say them out loud.
    - Ask your child these facts.
    - Have your child say, "Eleven" eleven times in response to your question because 6 + 5 = 11.
- Day 11+ worksheet
    - Have your child write this fact both ways on the first 11+ worksheet.
- Day 16 worksheet

Day 17
- Students will: practice known facts, compare weights, learn the math fact 6 + 6 = 12
- Practice the fact 6 + 6 = 12.
    - Have your child say it out loud to everyone in your home.
- Day 11+ worksheet.
    - Have your child add it to the 11+ worksheet. They can write it once or twice. It's up to them. It's the same both ways!
- Day 17 worksheet

Day 18
- Students will: practice known subtraction facts, compare numbers to 1000, learn the math fact $7 + 2 = 9$
- Have your child figure out what $7 + 2$ equals by counting on. They can hold out two fingers and count up from 7, "eight, nine."
  - Ask your child what $2 + 7$ is then.
  - Have your child stomp 9 times and say the problems out loud.
- Day 11+ worksheet
  - Have your child write the fact both ways on the 11+ page of the workbook.
- Day 18 worksheet
- Quiz your child on their subtraction facts.

Day 19 (crayon)
- Students will: count by 100s to 1000, practice known addition facts
- Does your child remember what $7 + 2$ equals?
- Day 19 worksheet

Day 20
- Students will: practice known subtraction facts, order numbers, learn the fact $7 + 3 = 10$
- Have your child figure out what $7 + 3$ equals by counting on.
  - Ask your child what $3 + 7$ equals.
  - Have your child say both facts out loud.
  - Ask your child how much $7 + 3$ is and have them jump the answer.
    - Jump 10 times.
- Day 11+ worksheet
  - Have your child write the fact both ways on the 11+ facts page in the workbook.
- Day 20 worksheet
- Quiz your child on known subtraction facts.

Addition Facts/Odd and Even Numbers

Day 21 (crayons)
- Students will: practice known addition facts, count by 1s, 10s, 100s
- Day 21 worksheet

Day 22 (eleven blocks or coins or something similar to count)
- Students will: identify odd numbers, recognize how many numbers can add up to eleven, learn the math fact $7 + 4 = 11$
- Continued…

- Review odd and even with your child.
  - Take out the 11 things you've gathered. Have your child divide them up between you and them: one to you, one to them, etc.
  - Ask your child if the final amounts are even.
    - They aren't. One has more than the other.
    - Eleven is an odd number.
  - Ask what needs to be done to make it even.
    - If you take one away from the pile with six, they will both have five.
    - How many are there all together?
      - Ten is an even number.
  - Continue to take away one and call the total number odd or even.
    - 9 is odd; 8 is even; 7 is odd; 6 is even, etc.
- Ask your child to figure out $7 + 4 = 11$.
  - Ask your child what $4 + 7$ equals.
  - Have your child say the equation out loud each way.
  - Have your child tell everyone in the house the equations.
- Day 11+ worksheet
  - Have your child write their new fact both ways on the 11+ worksheet
- Get out 11 blocks or coins or something.
  - Separate them into two piles with seven in one pile and four in the other. That shows that seven plus four equals eleven.
  - Now move one from the seven pile to the four pile. You should have six in one pile and five in the other. That shows that six plus five equals eleven.
  - Separate the piles into more ways. $9 + 2 = 11$, $10 + 1$… There are many ways to add up to eleven.
- Day 22 worksheet

Day 23
- Students will: practice known facts, learn the math fact $7 + 5 = 12$
- Learn $5 + 7$ and $7 + 5$.
  - Have your child figure out $7 + 5$. They can count on to add.
  - Ask your child what $5 + 7$ is.
  - Have your child say both equations out loud.
  - Have your child jump the answer.
    - Jump 12 times because $5 + 7 = 12$.
- Day 11+ worksheet
  - Have your child write the equation both ways on the 11+ worksheet page.
- Day 23 worksheet
- Quiz your child on their subtraction facts.

Day 24 (crayons)
- Students will: identify even numbers, practice known addition facts, learn the math fact $7 + 6 = 13$
- Ask your child if 2 is an even number.
  - It is.
- Have your child count by twos starting from two.
  - All of those numbers are even.
- Teach your child $7 + 6$ and have your child answer $6 + 7$.
- Have your child practice the new facts out loud.
- Ask your child what $7 + 6$ and $6 + 7$ are and have them clap the answer.
  - Clap 13 times because $7 + 6$ is 13.
- Day 11+ worksheet
  - Have your child fill in the fact both ways on one of the Day 11+ worksheets.
- Day 24 worksheet

Day 25
- Students will: practice known facts, learn the facts $7 + 7$, $8 + 8$, $9 + 9$
- Practice $7 + 7 = 14$, $8 + 8 = 16$, and $9 + 9 = 18$.
  - Say them out loud.
  - Draw a picture of them.
  - Run in place while repeating them.
  - Sing a song about them.
  - Whatever helps ☺
- Day 11+ worksheet
  - Write them on your facts worksheet.
- Day 25 worksheet
- Quiz your child on subtraction facts.

Comparing Numbers / Counting to 1000

Day 26 (crayon)
- Students will: practice known addition facts, identify patterns
- Turn to Day 19 in the workbook. Look for patterns. Can your child see what numbers stay the same in a row or column and which numbers change?
- Have your child color in the column and row with 3s in it. What's the pattern?
- Day 26 worksheet

Day 27
- Students will: add to ten, read number words, practice known addition facts, learn the math fact $8 + 2 = 10$
- Ask your child to figure out what $8 + 2$ is.
  - Practice $8 + 2$ and $2 + 8$ out loud several times.
- Continued…

- Ask your child to add to ten.
  - Nine plus what equals ten?
    - one
  - Eight plus what equals ten?
    - two
    - That's what you're learning today.
  - Seven plus what equals ten?
    - three
  - Six plus what equals ten?
    - four
  - Five plus what equals ten?
    - five
  - Four plus what equals ten?
    - six
  - Three plus what equals ten?
    - seven
  - Two plus what equals ten?
    - eight
  - One plus what equals ten?
    - nine
- Day 11+ worksheet
  - Have your child add $8 + 2 = 10$ and $2 + 8 = 10$ to their 11+ workbook page.
- Day 27 worksheet

Day 28
- Students will: practice known facts, identify numbers that come before and after up to 100, learn the math fact $8 + 3 = 11$.
- Practice your new fact.
  - Count on to find $8 + 3$.
  - Ask your child what $3 + 8$ is.
  - Have your child say the equations out loud.
  - Ask your child what $8 + 3$ and $3 + 8$ are and have your child stamp the answer.
    - Stamp 11 times because $8 + 3$ is 11.
- Day 11+ worksheet
  - Have your child fill in the new fact both ways on the Day 11+ worksheet.
- Day 28 worksheet
- Quiz your child on subtraction facts.

Day 29
- Students will: practice known addition facts, identify numbers that come before and after up to 1000, learn the math fact $8 + 4 = 12$
- Learn your new fact.
  - Have your child count on to figure out $8 + 4$.
  - Ask your child what $4 + 8$ is.
  - Have your child say the equations out loud.
  - Ask your child what $8 + 4$ and $4 + 8$ is and have your child clap the answer.
    - Clap 12 times because $8 + 4 = 12$.
- Day 11+ worksheet
  - Have your child fill in the new fact both ways on the Day 11+ workbook page.
- Day 29 worksheet

Day 30
- Students will: practice known addition facts, compare numbers to 1000
- Day 30 worksheet

Day 31
- Students will: practice known facts
- Review with your child: $7 + 5 = 12$, $7 + 6 = 13$, $7 + 7 = 14$
  - See if your child knows the answers and practice with forgotten facts by having your child repeat them and jump or sing or draw the answers.
- Day 31 worksheet

Day 32
- Students will: count by fives, identify and complete patterns, practice known addition facts, learn the addition fact $8 + 5 = 13$
- Practice counting by fives.
  - Have your child count by fives.
  - Have your child say five more when you give a number such as 50 and 25.
  - Let your child quiz you too.
- Teach your child the new fact.
  - Let your child hold out five fingers and use them to count on from eight to get to thirteen.
  - Ask your child what $5 + 8$ is.
  - Have your child repeat both facts out loud.
- Day 11+ worksheet
  - Add the fact both ways on the Day 11+ workbook pages.
- Day 32 worksheet

Day 33
- Students will: count by tens, practice known addition facts, learn the addition fact $8 + 6 = 14$
- Have your child count by tens from 400 to 500.
- Teach your child the new fact. Practice it both ways out loud. Quiz each other on the answer to both equations. Have your child share their new fact with someone.
- Day 11+ worksheet
  - Have your child add the fact both ways onto the Day 11+ workbook pages.
- Day 33 worksheet
- Quiz your child on subtraction facts.

Day 34
- Students will: count by tens, practice known addition facts, learn the addition fact $8 + 7 = 15$
- Have your child count by tens from 550 to 650.
- Teach your child the new fact. Practice it both ways out loud. Quiz each other. Have your child wiggle their nose fifteen times because $8 + 7 = 15$.
- Day 11+ worksheet
  - Have your child add the fact both ways on one of the Day 11+ workbook pages.
- Day 34 worksheet

Day 35
- Students will: practice with known facts
- Quiz your child and have your child quiz you on addition and subtraction facts.
- Day 35 worksheet

Addition Facts

Day 36
- Students will: practice with known facts
- Quiz your child and have your child quiz you on addition and subtraction facts.
- Day 36 worksheet
  - There's a new type of addition activity on their page that might throw them off at first. There is an example in the first stack. Each hexagon will be the answer when you add together the two numbers that are touching the bottom of it. The first one has the example of $4 + 4 = 8$.

Day 37
- Students will: practice known facts, learn the addition fact $9 + 2 = 11$
- Have your child count on to find the answer to $9 + 2$.
- Ask your child what is $2 + 9$ and have your child say the equation both ways out loud.
- Have your child blink the answer when you ask what is $2 + 9$ and $9 + 2$.
- Day 11+ worksheet
  - Have your child add the fact both ways on one of the Day 11+ worksheets.
- Day 37 worksheet
  - The bottom of the page has an activity where they add AND subtract. Point it out to your child, so they don't try to add the whole thing. They have to pay attention each time and either add or subtract.
- Quiz your subtraction facts.

Day 38 (optional: crayon)
- Students will: practice known facts, count backward from ten, learn the addition fact $9 + 3 = 12$
- Encourage your child that they almost know all the addition facts. Once they get to $9 + 9$ they will be able to add any number!
- Have your child count backward from ten.
- Have your child count on to figure out $9 + 3$.
- Practice $9 + 3$ and $3 + 9$ out loud.
- Ask your child to flap their arms to tell you the answer to $9 + 3$ and $3 + 9$.
- Day 11+ worksheet
  - Have your child fill in the fact both ways on one of the Day 11+ workbook pages.
- Day 38 worksheet
  - I thought it might help your child to write the answer to problems at the bottom of the page in crayon over top of the problems to help them remember where they are as they count down and work their way through the maze.
  - Again, this has addition and subtraction. You might want to point that out to your child.

Day 39 (coins or something to count)
- Students will: practice known addition facts, learn the fact $9 + 4 = 13$
- See if this helps your child with the 9 facts.
  - Lay out 15 coins (or whatever you have).
  - Have your child put ten together and five together.
  - Ask your child ten plus five.
    - 15
    - Your child can count to make sure if they aren't confident.
- Continued…

- o Move coins from pile to pile and ask your child how many coins there are.
  - It doesn't matter how many coins are in which pile, there are always 15 coins.
- o Put them back as ten and five. Have your child take one coin from the ten pile and add it to the five pile. Ask your child how many are in each pile.
  - 9 and 6
- o Ask your child how much is 9 + 6.
  - 15
- o Make the piles 10 and 4. Ask your child what is 10 + 4.
  - Have your child move one coin from the ten to the four pile and ask how many are in each pile.
    - 9 and 5
    - Ask your child what 9 + 5 is.
      - o 14
- o Make the piles 10 and 3. Ask your child what 10 and 3 are and then have your child take one away from ten and move it to the other pile. What math fact do the penny piles show?
  - 9 + 4 = 13
- o That's our math fact today. Nine plus any number is one less than that number plus ten.
- Practice your new facts 9 + 4 = 13 and 4 + 9 = 13.
- Ask your child to nod the answer to 9 + 4 and 4 + 9.
  - o Nod 13 times because 9 + 4 is 13.
- Day 11+ worksheet
  - o Have your child add the fact both ways to one of the Day 11+ workbook pages.
- Day 39 worksheet

Day 40
- Students will: practice known facts
- Quiz your child on subtraction facts.
- Day 40 worksheet

Day 41
- Students will: practice known addition facts, learn the fact 9 + 5 = 14
- See if your child can figure out 9 + 5.
- Quiz each other on your new facts.
- Have your child bend their knees and bounce the answer to 5 + 9.
- Day 11+ worksheet
  - o Have your child fill in the facts on one of the Day 11+ workbook pages.
- Day 41 worksheet

Day 42
- Students will: practice known facts, learn the fact $9 + 6 = 15$
- Quiz your child on subtraction facts.
- See if your child can figure out $9 + 6$.
- Practice your new facts together. Make sure your child is saying it out loud both ways and even telling others.
- You could have your child fake burp or sing "la" the number of the answer to $6 + 9$.
- Day 11+ worksheet
   - Add the facts to the facts page.
- Day 42 worksheet

Day 43
- Students will: practice known facts
- Quiz your subtraction facts.
- Day 43 worksheet

Day 44
- Students will: practice known addition facts, learn the fact $9 + 7 = 16$
- Encourage your child that they only have two more addition facts to learn and they will know them all!
- Can your child figure out $9 + 7$?
- Practice your new facts out loud several times.
- Dance for sixteen seconds because $9 + 7 = 16$.
- Day 11+ worksheet
   - Add your facts to your facts page.
- Day 44 worksheet

Day 45
- Students will: practice known facts
- Day 45 worksheet

Day 46
- Students will: practice known addition facts, learn the fact $9 + 8 = 17$
- See if your child can figure out $9 + 8$.
- Practice your new facts out loud. Have your child shout "yeah" the number of the answer to $8 + 9$.
- Day 11+ worksheet
   - Add these facts to your facts page.
- Day 46 worksheet

Day 47
- Students will: practice known facts
- You know all your facts! Congratulations! Do a happy dance. ☺
- Day 47 worksheet
- Quiz your subtraction facts.

Day 48
- Students will: use a number line to add with ten, practice known facts
- Day 48 worksheet
  - Help your child if necessary to know how to use the number line on the worksheet page for today. Does your child see the pattern with adding to ten?

Day 49
- Students will: practice known facts
- Day 49 worksheet
  - This is a maze that uses addition and subtraction.

Day 50
- Students will: practice known facts
- Day 50 worksheet
  - This is a maze that uses addition and subtraction.

Tens and Ones/Place Value

Day 51 (connecting blocks)
- Students will: be introduced to the concept of tens and ones, practice known facts
- Introduce tens and ones
  - Get out twenty blocks. It works best if they connect like Duplos or something like that.
  - Have your child count out ten blocks and then connect them all together into a tower of ten and then repeat with the other ten.
  - Ask your child how many groups of ten you have.
    - 2
  - Write the number twenty.
    - You have twenty blocks.
    - Show your child the number two. It means there are two tens and zero left over.
  - Take five of the blocks away. Ask your child how many groups of ten are there.
    - 1
  - How many single blocks are left over?
    - 5
    - We call those ones. There are five ones.
  - Continued…

- o Write the number fifteen.
  - 15
  - Show your child there are fifteen altogether.
  - Show your child the 1 in fifteen. Does that show the number of tens or the number of ones?
    - tens
    - There is one group of ten in fifteen.
  - Show your child the 5 in fifteen. Does that show the number of tens or ones?
    - ones
    - There are five ones in fifteen.
- o Decide if you want to do another example.
- Day 51 worksheet
- Day 51+ worksheet
  - o Do the first line on the worksheet.

Day 52 (scissors)
- Students will: practice with tens and ones, practice known facts
- Cut out the tens and ones blocks for Day 52.
- Have your child make 54 and 26 with the blocks and then any numbers they like.
  - o If you are able to hold onto these, you could use them on Day 65.
- Day 52 worksheet (after the cutouts)
- Day 51+ worksheet – Complete the next line on the page.

Day 53
- Students will: practice with tens and ones, practice known facts
- Day 53 worksheet
- Day 51+ worksheet – Complete the next line on the page.

Day 54
- Students will: practice with tens and ones, practice known facts
- Day 54 worksheet
- Day 51+ worksheet – Complete the next line on the page.

Day 55
- Students will: practice with tens and ones, practice known facts
- Day 55 worksheet
- Day 51+ worksheet – Complete the last line on the page.

Day 56
- Students will: practice with tens and ones, practice known facts
- Day 56 worksheet
- Day 56+ worksheet – Complete the first line on the page.

Day 57
- Students will: practice with tens and ones, practice known facts
- Day 57 worksheet
- Day 56+ worksheet – Complete the next line on the page.

Shapes

Day 58 (crayons, scissors, optional to have other paper and glue)
- Students will: identify 2D shapes, practice known facts
- Turn with your child to the Day 58 page in their workbook.
    - Ask your child which shapes they know.
    - Read the names of the others to your child.
    - Count sides together and find what makes each shape different from the others.
- Day 58 worksheet
    - The first page they will color the matching shape.
    - There is a second page for you to cut out the shapes.
    - Your child can make a picture or pictures from the shapes. They can move them into many different designs, or they could glue them into one picture.
- Day 56+ worksheet – Complete the next line on the page.

Day 59
- Students will: identify 3D shapes, practice known facts
- Sit with your child while they work on the Day 59 worksheet. There are some words on there that are new to them. They will start at the top of the list and do what they know and then figure out anything new.
    - A cuboid is a rectangular prism, a rectangular cube if you will.
- Day 59 worksheet
- Day 56+ worksheet – Do the next line on the page.

Day 60
- Students will: identify 2D shapes, practice known facts
- Day 60 worksheet
- Day 56+ worksheet – Do the last line on the page.
- Quiz the addition facts.

Subtraction Facts

Day 61 (coins, or anything you can count and move around)
- Students will: recognize the "family relationship" between addition and subtraction facts, practice known facts, learn facts $8 - 2 = 6$ and $9 - 3 = 6$
- Time to get out the coins again or blocks or whatever you'd like to work with.
    - Take out 9 coins.
    - Have your child take away 3 and count how many remain.
        - 6
    - Ask your child how many there would be if you put them all back together into one pile.
        - 9
        - because $3 + 6 = 9$
    - Put them all back together and have your child take away 6 and count how many remain.
        - 3
    - Ask how many would be in the pile if they were all put back together.
        - 9, Why?
            - $6 + 3 = 9$
    - Ask your child to see how addition and subtraction are opposites.
- We call 3, 6, and 9 a fact family. $3 + 6 = 9$, $6 + 3 = 9$, $9 - 3 = 6$, $9 - 6 = 3$
- Write this family and the addition and subtraction equations they make on the first Day 61+ fact family sheet.
    - The nine will go in the top circle, the three and six underneath. Show your child with the triangle how those numbers add and subtract to get each as the answer.
    - Fill in the equation lines with two addition and two subtraction equations made from this fact family.
- Take away one coin. Have your child count how many coins you have.
    - Ask your child to take two coins out of the pile and count how many remain.
    - See if your child can tell you the fact family.
        - 2, 6, 8
    - Add this to your Day 61+ fact family page.
        - $2 + 6 = 8$, $6 + 2 = 8$, $8 - 2 = 6$, $8 - 6 = 2$
- Day 61 worksheet

Day 62
- Students will: practice known facts, spelling of numbers, learn the fact families of 4, 6, 10 and 5, 6, 11
- Day 61+ fact family page
    - Add the two new fact families.
    - Have your child say these subtraction facts out loud.
- Day 62 worksheet
    - Your child may need help finding the words in the word search.

Day 63 (Grab a square block or a die, a box, a cylinder shape of some sort, a ball, and a pyramid shape if you can find one.)
- Students will: practice known subtraction facts, learn geometric terminology of edges, faces, vertices and use them to describe objects
- Show your child the block and introduce these terms.
    - A face is a flat side. Count the faces on the block together.
        - 6, That's why dice have 6 numbers on them.
        - Figure out together how many faces a cylinder has. (If you don't have a cylinder, just roll up a piece of paper.)
            - 2
            - The top and bottom are flat. The curved middle is not a flat side.
        - How many faces does a ball have?
            - 0
            - There are no flat sides.
        - Give your child the box and ask them to count the faces.
            - 6
    - A vertex is a point. If there are more than one, then there are vertices. (Say ver-tuh-seez.)
        - Count the vertices on the block.
            - 8, each corner
        - Count the vertices on the cylinder and the sphere, the ball.
            - 0
        - Have your child count the number of vertices on the box.
            - 8
    - An edge is the sharp line edge between two faces. It's a line between two vertices.
        - Count the edges on your block.
            - 12
        - How many edges do your sphere and cylinder have?
            - none
            - If there aren't two vertices, there can't be any edges.
- Day 63 worksheet

Day 64
- Students will: practice addition facts, work with the fact families 6, 7, 13 and 6, 8, 14
- Day 61+ fact family sheet
    - Add these new facts.
    - Have your child say the new subtraction facts out loud and practice however works best for your child to help them remember.
- Day 64 worksheet

Day 65 (You could use your tens and ones paper blocks today.)
- Students will: identify numbers as tens and ones, learn the fact families of 6, 9, 15 and 7, 2, 9
- If you have your tens and ones paper blocks, make more numbers. Identify the total, the tens, and the ones. Ask your child to make certain numbers like 37 and 82.
  - You could hold onto these if you want. You'll be adding and subtracting tens and ones toward the end of the year.
- Day 61+ fact family sheet
  - Add your new fact families for today.
  - Have your child say the new subtraction facts out loud.
  - If your child can't remember an answer, encourage them to use addition to help figure it out.
    - What plus 2 equals 9? To help with the answer to 9 – 2.
- Day 65 worksheet

Day 66
- Students will: practice known subtraction facts, learn fact families 7, 3, 10 and 7, 4, 11
- Day 61 + worksheet
  - Add your new fact families.
  - Have your child say the new subtraction facts out loud and quiz each other on them.
- Day 66 worksheet

Day 67
- Students will: practice known addition facts, learn fact families 7, 5, 12 and 7, 8, 15
- Day 61+ worksheet
  - Add your new fact families and practice the new subtraction facts.
  - Remember that you can use your addition facts to help you figure out your subtraction facts.
- Day 67 worksheet

Day 68 (crayon)
- Students will: identify even numbers, practice known subtraction facts
- Have your child read out loud all of the subtraction equations from the fact family pages (61+) .
- Day 68 worksheet
  - They will color in the even numbered answers.

Day 69
- Students will: practice addition facts, learn fact families 7, 9, 16 and 7, 7, 14
- Day 61+ worksheet
  - Add your new fact families to your page.
  - Practice your new subtraction facts.
- Day 69 worksheet

Day 70 (crayon)
- Students will: identify odd numbers, practice subtraction facts, learn fact families 8, 2, 10 and 8, 3, 11
- Day 61+ worksheet
  - Add the new fact families to your facts page.
  - Practice the new subtraction facts out loud.
- Day 70 worksheet
  - They will color in the odd answers.

Day 71
- Students will: practice known subtraction facts, learn the fact families 8, 4, 12 and 8, 5, 13
- Day 61+ worksheet
  - Add your new fact families to the page.
  - Practice your new subtraction facts.
- Day 71 worksheet

Day 72
- Students will: practice addition facts, learn the facts families 9, 2, 11 and 9, 3, 12
- Day 61+ worksheet
  - Add your new fact families to your page.
  - Practice your new subtraction facts.
- Day 72 worksheet
  - You might need to help your child with the directions on this page.

Day 73
- Students will: practice fact families
- Read your fact family pages; do it like this. Say, "Fifteen minus seven is," and then jump eight times. Jump, stomp, clap, wiggle, blink, do push ups, turn in circles, etc. for all of the answers. Don't cheat. Do them all!
- Day 73 worksheet

Day 74
- Students will: practice addition facts, learn fact families 9, 4, 13 and 9, 5, 14
- Day 61+ worksheet
  - Add your new fact families.
  - Practice your new subtraction facts.
- Day 74 worksheet
  - Use the example to show your child how to solve the addition squares.

Day 75
- Students will: practice known subtraction facts, learn fact families 8, 8, 16 and 8, 9, 17
- Day 61+ worksheet
  - Add your new fact families to your page.
  - Practice your new subtraction facts.
- Day 75 worksheet

Day 76
- Students will: practice addition and subtraction facts, learn fact families 6, 6, 12 and 9, 9, 18
- These are the last subtraction facts. Encourage your child that they know it all now and will be amazing as they add and subtract anything in the world.
- 61+ worksheet
  - Add these last facts to your page.
  - Practice these facts.
- Day 76 worksheet
  - Make sure your child realizes there are both addition and subtraction problems.

Day 77
- Students will: practice addition and subtraction facts
- Day 77 worksheet
  - Again make sure your child stops to look if they are supposed to add or subtract.

Day 78 (scissors, glue or tape)
- Students will: practice identifying parts of 3D shapes
- Day 78 worksheet
  - Cut out the cube and pyramids and make them.
- Count the number of faces, edges, and vertices.
  - Cube: 6 faces, 8 vertices, 12 edges
  - Pyramid with square base: 5 faces, 5 vertices, 8 edges
  - Triangular Pyramid: 4 faces, 4 vertices, 6 edges
- You can describe a shape to each other using these terms and guess which shape it is.

Day 79
- Students will: identify shapes, practice subtraction facts
- Day 79 worksheet

Day 80
- Students will: practice addition and subtraction facts
- Day 80 worksheet
- Quiz your child on subtraction facts.

Word Problems

Day 81
- Students will: practice addition facts, learn to solve word problems
- We're going to work through an example of a word problem together.
- Let's say you have six people in your family. Another family with four people in it come over for dinner. How many people will be sitting at the table?
  - That's a word problem. You need to figure out the answer, so you know how many chairs and plates you'll need to set up.
  - How do you figure it out? You have 6 people plus 4 more come. That's 6 plus 4. $6 + 4 = 10$ That's your answer.
- Day 81 worksheet
  - Read the first word problem on the page with your child.
  - Mark rode his bike 7 miles to the library.
  - He then rode to the park 5 miles away.
  - How many miles did Mark ride altogether?
    - I'm going to give you a hint. When a problem says altogether, you are going to add to find your answer. Before we add, let's start with a picture.
  - Take a piece of paper. Draw Mark on one side. Draw a library on the other side (it can just be a square.) Then draw a tree for the park. Put your finger on Mark. Your finger is Mark. Now move your finger up and over and to the library.
  - How far did Mark go so far? How many miles?
    - Read the problem to find out.
    - answer: 7 miles Write the number seven on the paper in the first blank in the equation on the right side.
  - Now move your finger straight to the park. How far did Mark go to get there? Look at the problem and find the number.
    - answer: 5 miles
    - Write the number five in the next blank in the equation.
- Continued…

- o Now let's do it altogether. Put your finger on Mark. Go 7 miles to the library and 5 miles to the park. How far did Mark go altogether?
  - ▪ He went 7 miles plus 5 miles more. Write a plus sign between the 7 and the 5 in the circle.
- o What's the answer? Fill in the rest of the blanks.
  - ▪ Now, he didn't go 12 centimeters or 12 feet. He went 12 miles. In a word problem it is VERY important to label your answer, write the word that you are talking about (like miles for this problem).
- You solved your first word problem. Way to go! Now you can play a game.
- Finish the Day 81 worksheet
- Day 81+ worksheet – Do the first line on the page.

Day 82 (optional: coins or something for counting – 10 of them)
- Students will: practice subtraction facts, learn to solve word problems
- Let's practice another word problem.
  - o Anne ate 6 cookies. Samantha ate 4 more cookies than Anne. How many cookies did Samantha eat?
  - o Draw a picture or use coins as cookies. You need 6 cookies. Draw 6 cookies or lay out 6 "cookies."
- Who ate that many cookies?
  - o Anne
- Who ate the most cookies? Read the problem carefully to find the answer.
  - o Samantha
- The problem tells us that Samantha ate more cookies than Anne.
- How many cookies did Samantha eat? How do we figure it out? We know she ate 6 cookies, just like Anne, but then she ate more. How many more?
  - o answer: 4 more
- Add 4 more cookies to your drawing or lego collection.
- How many cookies did Samantha eat? What's the number equation? That means the problem with numbers and no words.
  - o answer: $6 + 4 =$
- How many cookies?
  - o answer: 10 cookies
  - o Make sure to label your answers.
- Day 82 worksheet
- Day 81+ worksheet – Do the next line on the workbook page.

Day 83
- Students will: practice known addition facts, learn to solve word problems
- Let's work through another word problem.
  - Henry gave 5 stickers to his younger brother. Now he only has 9 stickers. How many stickers did Henry have at first?
  - What should we do first? Let's draw a picture.
    - Draw two people. Draw one stick person on one side of the page and another stick person on the other side of the page.
  - Draw 5 stickers under one and 9 stickers under the other.
  - How many stickers does Henry have now?
    - answer: 9 stickers
  - Before he had those nine stickers plus all of the stickers he gave his brother. What's this word problem as an equation, as a number problem?
    - answer: $9 + 5 =$
  - How many stickers did Henry have at first, before he gave any away?
    - 14 stickers
    - Make sure to use the word stickers.
- Remind your child to label their answers.
- Day 83 worksheet
- Day 81+ worksheet – Do the next line on the page.

Day 84 (optional: coins or something for counting – 15 of them)
- Students will: practice known subtraction facts, learn to solve word problems
- Talk through another word problem.
  - Derek and Larry have 15 books together. 6 of the books belong to Derek. How many books does Larry have?
  - What do we do first?
    - answer: Draw a picture.
  - Draw a picture of 15 books. (You can just make a line for each book. It doesn't have to be a pretty picture.) Or, you can get out 15 coins and pretend they are the books.
  - Your fifteen books are Derek's and Larry's. Right now they are all together in one big pile.
  - How many of the books are Derek's?
    - answer: 6 books
  - Count out six coins and put them in a separate pile. Or, circle six books in your picture. Those are the ones that belong to Derek.
  - Who do the rest of the books belong to?
    - answer: Larry
  - So, how many books does Larry have? Count them up. That's the answer.
  - But how do we get that with a number problem? What kind of problem is it when you have a lot and then take some away? Is it an addition problem or a subtraction problem?
    - answer: subtraction
- Continued…

- o What is this word problem as a number problem?
  - answer: $15 - 6 =$
- o How many books does Larry have?
  - 9 books
- Day 84 worksheet
- Day 81+ worksheet – Do the next line on the page.

Day 85

- Students will: practice known facts, solve word problems
- Day 85 worksheet
  - o If your child doesn't know how to solve the problem, remind them to start with a picture of the problem.
- Day 81+ worksheet – Do the last line on the page.

Day 86

- Students will: practice known facts, solve word problems
- Day 86 worksheet
  - o If your child doesn't know how to solve the problem, remind them to start with a picture of the problem.
- Day 86+ worksheet – Do the first line on the page.

Day 87

- Students will: practice known facts, solve word problems
- Day 87 worksheet
  - o If your child doesn't know how to solve the problem, remind them to start with a picture of the problem.
- Day 86+ worksheet – Do the next line on the page.

Day 88

- Students will: practice known facts, solve word problems
- Day 88 worksheet
  - o If your child doesn't know how to solve the problem, remind them to start with a picture of the problem.
- Day 86+ worksheet – Do the next line on the page.

Day 89

- Students will: practice known facts, solve word problems
- Day 89 worksheet
  - o If your child doesn't know how to solve the problem, remind them to start with a picture of the problem.
- Day 86+ worksheet – Do the next line on the page.

Day 90
- Students will: practice known facts, solve word problems
- Day 90 worksheet
  - If your child doesn't know how to solve the problem, remind them to start with a picture of the problem.
- Day 86+ worksheet – Do the next line on the page.

Money

Day 91 (brown crayon, coins)
- Students will: practice known facts, identify coins and their value
- Get out some coins including a penny, nickel, dime, and quarter.
  - Have your child arrange them into groups.
  - See what your child knows about how much they are worth and what's worth more.
  - Have your child investigate the pictures on the front and backs of the coins.
  - Tell your child what they are worth.
- Day 91 worksheet
- Day 91+ worksheet – Do the first line of the worksheet.
- Quiz subtraction facts. Keep working on facts with quizzing, flashcards, games, facts practice books.

Day 92 (coins – dimes, nickels, pennies, at least a few of each if you can)
- Students will: practice known facts, count the value of a group of coins including dimes, nickels, and pennies
- Get out a handful of coins and have your child organize them into groups of like coins.
- Practice counting the value of coins.
  - Count the value of the pennies. Each penny is worth 1 cent, so you count 1 for each penny.
    - 5 pennies = 5 cents
  - Count the value of the dimes. Each dime is worth 10 cents, so you count 10 for each dime.
    - 5 dimes = 50 cents 10, 20, 30, 40, 50
  - Count the value of the nickels. Each nickel is worth 5 cents, so you count 5 for each nickel.
    - 5 nickels = 25 cents 5, 10, 15, 20, 25
  - Choose some coins from each pile and count the value together. Start with the highest value, the dimes, then add on the nickels, then the pennies.
    - 2 dimes, 3 nickels, 2 pennies
    - 10, 20, 25, 30, 35, 36, 37
- Continued…

- Day 92 worksheet
  - If it helps your child, there is a hundreds chart on the page they can use to help them count on.
- Day 91+ worksheet – Do the next line on the worksheet.
- Quiz your addition facts.

Day 93 (coins – four quarters as well as dimes, nickels, pennies)
- Students will: count the value of a group of coins including quarters, practice known facts
- Take out four quarters. Have your child look at them. Teach your child how to count quarters: 25, 50, 75, 100.
  - Have your child practice counting quarters.
  - Teach your child that 100 equals 1 dollar.
  - Ask your child how much would be one quarter and one dime.
    - Practice counting by tens starting at 25. You could use the hundreds chart on the page for Day 92 for a visual of counting by tens not starting at 10.
- Put coins together and help your child count the value. Again, start with the highest value, the quarter. Then count on the dimes.
- Day 93 worksheet
- Day 91+ worksheet – Do the next line on the worksheet.
- Quiz your subtraction facts.

Day 94 (brown crayon, optional: coins)
- Students will: count the value of a group of coins, practice facts
- If you want, practice counting coins together again.
- Day 94 worksheet
- Day 91+ worksheet – Do the next line on the worksheet.
- Quiz your addition facts.

Day 95 (coins)
- Students will: discriminate between coins and add their quantity and value
- Day 95 worksheet
  - Your child will need a pile of coins including quarters, dimes, nickels, pennies.
- Day 91+ worksheet – Do the last line on the worksheet.
- Quiz your subtraction facts.

Day 96 (brown crayon, optional: penny, nickel, dime, quarter)
- Students will: practice facts, count the value of coins, identify missing coin
- Day 96 worksheet
  - Your child will be figuring out which one more coin needs to be included to make the total 25 cents. If your child isn't sure which coin, have your child try each coin, adding it on to see how much it would be. They could even place a coin in the line and add its value together with the other coins.
- Day 96+ worksheet – Do the first line on the worksheet.

Day 97 (brown crayon)
- Students will: practice facts, count the value of a group of coins
- Day 97 worksheet
- Day 96+ worksheet – Do the next line on the worksheet.

Day 98 (brown crayon)
- Students will: practice facts, count the value of a group of coins and compare it to the cost of an item
- Day 98 worksheet
- Day 96+ worksheet – Do the next line on the worksheet.

Day 99 (optional: coins)
- Students will: practice facts, find the fewest number of coins needed to purchase an item
- Day 99 worksheet
  - I suggest doing an example or the first one with your child. They will need to use the fewest number of coins. That means they should check the highest value coin first and work their way down.
  - The first item is worth 7 cents.
    - Have your child say if the quarter is too much.
      - It is.
    - Have your child check the next coin. What is it? What is it worth?
      - The dime is worth ten cents and it's more than what's needed.
    - Have your child check the next coin. What is it? What is it worth?
      - The nickel is worth five cents. It's less than seven, so you can use it.
      - Try another nickel. That would be how much?
        - 10 cents, but that's too much
      - So, we can use one nickel. Write 1 in the nickel column.
    - Now try the pennies. How many do you need to get to 7?
      - 2 more
      - Write 2 in the pennies column.
- Continued…

- o If it helps your child to have the visual, you can give your child coins to put together to add their value.
- Day 96+ worksheet – Do the next line on the worksheet.

Day 100
- Students will: practice facts, count the value of coins, find the fewest number of coins to make a certain amount
- Day 100 worksheet
- Day 96+ worksheet – Do the last line on the worksheet.

Word Problems

Day 101
- Students will: practice facts, solve word problems
- Day 101 worksheet
  - o If your child doesn't know how to solve a problem, encourage them to draw a picture or act it out.
- Day 101+ worksheet – Do the first line on the worksheet.

Day 102
- Students will: practice facts, solve word problems
- Day 102 worksheet
  - o If your child doesn't know how to solve a problem, encourage them to draw a picture or act it out.
  - o You can remind your child that the word "altogether" is a clue to add.
- Day 101+ worksheet – Do the next line on the worksheet.

Day 103
- Students will: practice facts, solve word problems
- Day 103 worksheet
  - o If your child doesn't know how to solve a problem, encourage them to draw a picture or act it out.
  - o You can tell your child that the word "less" is a clue to subtract.
- Day 101+ worksheet – Do the next line on the worksheet.

Day 104
- Students will: practice facts, solve word problems
- Day 104 worksheet
  - o If your child doesn't know how to solve a problem, encourage them to draw a picture or act it out.
- Day 101+ worksheet – Do the next line on the worksheet.

Day 105
- Students will: practice facts, solve word problems
- Day 105 worksheet
  - If your child doesn't know how to solve a problem, encourage them to draw a picture or act it out.
- Day 101+ worksheet – Do the last line on the worksheet.

Money

Day 106 (crayons, money: bills – ones, fives, tens and coins)
- Students will: identify ways to make a dollar, add the value of bills, practice facts
- Remind your child that one hundred cents is one dollar. Think together of all the ways you can make one dollar. Here are some.
  - 100 pennies are worth 1 dollar
  - 20 nickles are worth 1 dollar — 5, 10, 15, 20, 25, 30, 35, 40, 45, 50, 55, 60, 65, 70, 75, 80, 85, 90, 95, 100
  - 10 dimes are worth 1 dollar — 10, 20, 30, 40, 50, 60, 70, 80 90, 100
  - 4 quarters are worth 1 dollar — 25, 50, 75, 100
- Count the value of your bills together with your child. You can use play money or make your own.
  - Make sure you child understands five 1 dollar bills are worth the same amount of money as one 5 dollar bill.
  - In the same way, two five dollar bills are worth the same amount of money as one ten dollar bill. Right? 5 + 5 = 10 so $5 + $5 = $10
- Day 106 worksheet
- Day 106+ worksheet – Do the first line on the worksheet.

Day 107 (brown crayon)
- Students will: count the value of coins, practice facts
- Day 107 worksheet
- Day 106+ worksheet – Do the next line on the worksheet.

Day 108 (brown crayon)
- Students will: compare the value of coins, practice facts
- Day 108 worksheet
- Day 106+ worksheet – Do the next line on the worksheet.

Day 109 (brown crayon)
- Students will: count the value of bills and coins, practice facts
- Day 109 worksheet
- Day 106+ worksheet – Do the next line on the worksheet.

Day 110 (brown crayon)
- Students will: count the value of bills and coins, practice facts
- Day 110 worksheet
- Day 106+ worksheet – Do the last line on the worksheet.

Day 111 (optional: coins)
- Students will: solve money word problems, practice facts
- Day 111 worksheet
    - Your child might like to work with real coins to help solve the problems.
    - They will be doing money word problems for the next several days, and it's not all easy.
- Quiz your child on addition facts.

Day 112 (optional: coins)
- Students will: solve money word problems, practice facts
- Day 112 worksheet
- Quiz your child on subtraction facts.

Day 113 (optional: coins)
- Students will: solve money word problems, practice facts
- Day 113 worksheet
- Quiz your child on addition facts.

Day 114 (optional: coins)
- Students will: solve money word problems, practice facts
- Day 114 worksheet
- Quiz your child on subtraction facts.

Day 115
- Students will: practice known facts
- Day 115 worksheet

Time

Day 116 (crayons optional)
- Students will: tell time on analog clocks to the hour and half hour, practice facts
- Use the Day 116 worksheet to review time with your child. Does your child remember the hour hand and minute hand? Can your child show which clocks are on the hour and which are showing half an hour?
- Day 116 worksheet
- Day 116+ worksheet – Do the first line on the worksheet.

Day 117
- Students will: count minutes by five around a clock, practice facts
- Use the Day 116 page to talk about the hour and minute hand.
  - When the hour hand is pointing directly at a number, it's exactly that time.
  - If the hour hand is past a number, then it's that hour plus some minutes have gone by.
  - The top of the page has times on the hour, so the hour hand points directly to the number.
  - On the bottom of the page the hour hands are between the numbers because it's halfway between the hours.
- Use the Day 117 worksheet to count the minutes around the clock.
  - Show your child that each line is one minute, but the big numbers show us every five minutes.
  - Have your child count the lines to ten minutes.
  - Tell your child it's faster to count by fives. Have your child touch the 1 and say, "Five," and the 2 and say, "Ten."
    - That's easier than trying to count the little lines.
    - It can help us read the time faster.
  - Have your child point to each number and count by fives around the clock. If done correctly, they should be at fifty-five when they touch the 11.
- Day 117 worksheet
- Day 116+ worksheet – Do the next line on the worksheet.

Day 118 (crayons optional)
- Students will: tell time to the quarter hour, practice facts
- Day 118 worksheet
  - Have your child count by fives around the clock to find out how many minutes have passed when the minute hand is pointing at the three and nine.
  - Use the workbook page to show your child what it looks like on a digital time to have fifteen or forty-five minutes.
- Day 116 + worksheet – Do the next line on the worksheet.

Day 119
- Students will: tell time to the quarter hour, practice facts
- Day 119 worksheet
  - Show your child on the worksheet how the hour hand starts at the number when the hour begins and then points after the number for the rest of the hour. The hour is always the number passed, not the next number coming up.
- Day 116+ worksheet – Do the next line on the worksheet.

Day 120 (crayons optional)
- Students will: tell time to 5 minutes, practice facts
- Day 120 worksheet
  - Have your child count by fives around the clock. Ask your child how many minutes have passed after the hour when the minute hand is pointing to the four.
    - 20
- Day 116+ worksheet – Do the last line on the worksheet.

Day 121
- Students will: tell time to 5 minutes, practice facts
- Day 121 worksheet
  - Remind your child or practice together counting around the clock by fives.
  - Remind your child that the hour hand is shorter and points after the hour.
  - They don't have to get precise about the hour hand placement, but for reading times, it's good to practice that the hour hand comes on after the hour.
- Day 121+ worksheet – Do the first row of problems.

Day 122
- Students will: calculate elapsed time, draw hands on clocks, practice facts
- Day 122 worksheet
  - Have your child write the time on the first clock. Then have them put their finger on the hour and count on or off the number of hours in the word problem to find the new time.
    - Only the hour will change. The minutes stay the same in each problem.
  - They will write the new time under the blank clock and then draw in the time.
- Day 121+ worksheet – Do the next line on the page.

Day 123
- Students will: calculate elapsed time, learn a.m. and p.m., practice facts
- You need to introduce the terms a.m. and p.m. to your child. They are abbreviations for Latin words which just mean before and after midday.
  - To start introduce noon and midnight. Does your child know when they are?
    - 12 p.m.
    - 12 a.m.
  - These divide our day in half. In a lot of places, they use 24 hour clocks. 4 p.m. is 16 o'clock in other parts of the world.
  - We say p.m., meaning after noon.
  - We say a.m., meaning morning, anytime between midnight and noon.
- Continued…

- Ask your child about different things in your day and if they happen in the a.m. or p.m.
  - waking up, dinner, bed time, breakfast, etc.
- Day 123 worksheet
  - Your child can use the previous page if they want to touch a clock to count the hours.
  - They will also circle a.m. or p.m. for most answers. This isn't tricky. It's not going to change from what's in the problem.
- Day 121+ worksheet – Do the next line on the page.

Day 124 (optional: die if you want to play as a game)
- Students will: tell time after 5 minutes has elapsed, practice facts
- Day 124 worksheet
  - This worksheet can be played as a game. Roll the die, move forward, tell the time and what the time will be in 5 minutes. Race to the end of the page.
  - Or, your child can read you the clocks and tell you what the time will be in five minutes.
  - Either way your child will just count on five to get the time five minutes later.
- Day 121+ worksheet – Do the next line on the page.

Day 125
- Students will: draw hands on clocks, find elapsed time with hours and half hours, practice facts
- Day 125 worksheet
  - You might want to sit with your child on this one depending on how confident they are. Encourage your child to touch the hour and count around the clock to find the new time.
  - They will be finding elapsed time and drawing the new time on clocks. Sometimes they will be adding a half hour to the time.
    - This is only going from like 3:00 to 3:30.
- Day 121+ worksheet – Do the last line on the page.

Day 126
- Students will: solve word problems, practice facts
- Day 126 worksheet
  - Remind your child that every answer needs a label. What is it they are finding? An amount of money, a number of books or hours?
- Day 126+ worksheet – Do the first line on the page.

Day 127 (brown crayon, optional: bills, coins)
- Students will: count the value of bills and coins, make amounts with the fewest number of coins
- Day 127 worksheet
  - If it would help your child, get out coins and bills to have them count up, especially to work out the fewest number of coins needed for the Part B.
  - Remind your child to always start counting with the largest amount.
- Day 126+ worksheet – Do the next line on the page.

Graphing

Day 128
- Students will: learn to read a graph, practice facts
- Day 128 worksheet. Use the worksheet to review graphs.
  - The top graph is a bar graph. Find:
    - the title: Pets on My Street
    - the labels: number of pets and type of pet
    - the scale: the numbers up the side
    - the bars: how much is filled in for each pet.
  - Answer the question. Count the bars filled in for birds.
    - 4 birds
  - The bottom graph is a pictograph. Find the title, labels, and key.
    - The key tells us how much each picture of a book represents.
      - Here each book represents 2 books.
      - One book picture means the kid read two books. Two pictures of books mean the kid read four books.
  - Answer the question. How many books did Sam read?
    - Count by twos and get 6 books.
- Day 126+ worksheet – Do the next line on the page.

Day 129 (crayons)
- Students will: create and read a bar graph, practice facts
- Day 129 worksheet
  - Do the first one, the cat, with your child to make sure they understand.
    - Count the tally marks, 7.
    - Color in 7 bars.
  - They will answer the questions once the graph is filled in.
- Day 126+ worksheet – Do the next line on the page.

Day 130 (crayons)
- Students will: create and read a bar graph, practice facts
- Day 130 worksheet
  - This is the same set up as Day 129.
- Day 126+ worksheet – Do the last line on the page.

Day 131 (crayons)
- Students will: create and read a bar graph, practice facts
- Day 131 worksheet
  - Have your child tell you what the graph will be showing.
- Day 131+ worksheet – Do the first line on the page.

Day 132
- Students will: read a pictograph, practice facts
- Day 132 worksheet
  - Have your child open to the Day 132 worksheet.
  - Have your child read the graph's title and key.
    - How many books does each picture represent?
      - 2 books
    - How many books is shown where there is half a book?
      - 1 book
  - Have your child use the graph to answer the questions.
- Day 131+ worksheet – Do the next line on the worksheet.

Day 133
- Students will: read a pictograph, practice facts
- Day 133 worksheet
  - Have your child open to the Day 133 worksheet.
  - Have your child read the graph's title and key.
    - How many apples does each picture represent?
      - 10 apples
    - How many apples are shown where there is half an apple?
      - 5 apples
  - Have your child use the graph to answer the questions.
    - They will be counting by tens when they count the apples.
- Day 131+ worksheet – Do the next line on the worksheet.

Day 134 (crayons, at least five colors)
- Students will: read a pictograph, practice facts
- Day 134 worksheet
  - Have your child find the title (favorite desserts) and the labels (the dessert names along the side).
  - They are going to create the key. They should color in each box next to a dessert name a different color.
  - To fill in the chart they will use the tally marks to know how many slices of the pie graph to color in.
- Continued…

- The first one is a slice of cake. Ask your child how many people chose the cake.
  - There are two tally marks.
  - They should color in two slices on the pie graph. This can also be called a circle graph or a pie chart.
  - Have your child complete the graph and answer the questions.
- Day 131+ worksheet – Do the next line on the worksheet.

Day 135
- Students will: collect data and use a bar graph to display it, practice facts
- Day 135 worksheet
  - Your child is going to create a bar graph. First, they need to decide what it will show.
    - Maybe they want to do one showing the vegetables or fruits and vegetables in the house and how many of each there are.
    - They could do money, blocks of different Lego colors, etc.
  - Each bar on the graph can represent one unless they want to get fancy.
- Day 131+ worksheet – Do the last line on the worksheet.

Fractions

Day 136 (crayons, coins or other object to count)
- Students will: identify half of a group of objects and half of a shape, practice facts
- Day 136 worksheet
  - Take out an even number of coins or other object and have your child split the group in half.
  - Depending on how comfortable your child is with it, they can do that several times or move on to the workbook.
- Day 136+ worksheet – Do the first line on the page.

Day 137 (crayons, four coins or other object to count)
- Students will: identify one quarter, one half, and three quarters of a group of objects and of a shape, practice facts
- Take out the four coins and have your child find:
  - one half of them
    - 2
  - a quarter of them, 1 out of 4
    - 1
  - three quarters of them, 3 out of 4
    - 3
  - This is why quarters are called quarters. They split a dollar into four parts, into quarters.
- Day 137 worksheet
- Day 136+ worksheet – Do the next line on the page.

Day 138 (crayons)
- Students will: identify thirds, understand that fractions are parts of a whole
- Put together six blocks or draw six blocks all connected.
  - Ask your child how many blocks the big rectangle is divided into.
    - 6
  - Each piece is one sixth.
  - Two pieces is two sixths.
  - Continue counting through the pieces: three sixths, four sixths, five sixths, six sixths
  - Six sixths or six out of the six parts is the whole thing.
- Take away three.
  - Go through the process again with three pieces.
    - How many pieces are there?
      - 3
    - How much is each one?
      - 1/3, one third
    - How much would two pieces be out of the whole?
      - two out of three parts, two thirds
- Day 138 worksheet
- Day 136+ worksheet – Do the next line on the page.

Day 139 (crayon)
- Students will: identify fractions from a representation, create representations of a fraction, read fractions as numbers, practice facts
- Turn to the Day 139 worksheet and read the fractions with your child.
- Make sure your child knows that the top number is the parts of the whole, how many are colored in, and that the bottom number is the total number of parts.
- Day 139 worksheet
- Day 136+ worksheet – Do the next line on the page.

Day 140 (crayon)
- Students will: identify fractions from a representation, create representations of a fraction, read fractions as numbers, practice facts
- Day 140 worksheet
  - Decide if your child needs more practice reading fractions.
  - Ask your child what the top and bottom numbers mean.
    - The bottom number is how many parts there are all together.
    - The top is how many are colored in, the parts of the whole.
- Day 136+ worksheet – Do the next line on the page.

Day 141
- Students will: identify fractions from a representation, write fractions, practice facts
- Day 141 worksheet
- Day 141+ worksheet – Do the first line on the page.

Day 142 (crayon)
- Students will: create representations of fractions, write fractions, practice facts
- Day 142 worksheet
- Have your child read the fractions in Part A.
- Day 141+ worksheet – Do the next line on the page.

Day 143 (crayon)
- Students will: create representations of fractions, write fractions, practice facts
- Day 143 worksheet
    - This has the fractions only as words. They will have to read the words and then write those as fractions.
- Day 141+ worksheet – Do the next line on the page.

Day 144
- Students will: read fractions as numbers and words, write fractions, practice facts
- Day 144 worksheet
- Day 141+ worksheet – Do the next line on the page.

Day 145
- Students will: identify representations of fractions, read fractions as numbers and words, practice facts
- Day 145 worksheet
- Day 141+ worksheet – Do the last line on the page.

Measurement

Day 146 (centimeter ruler)
- Students will: measure to the half centimeter, practice facts
- Look at the ruler with your child.
    - Show them the centimeter side. How long is the ruler?
    - Does the ruler show half centimeters? Where?
    - Show your child how to line up the zero with the edge of something to measure.
    - Use a finger to practice measuring something to the half centimeter. (Just move your finger some to make it end at a half centimeter.)
- Day 146 worksheet
- Day 146+ worksheet – Do the first line on the page.

Day 147 (inch ruler)
- Students will: measure to the quarter inch, practice facts
- Look at the ruler with your child.
    - Show them the inch side. How long is the ruler?
    - Does the ruler show half inches? Where?
    - Does the ruler show quarter inches? Where?
        - There should be longer lines showing half and quarter measurements.
    - Show your child how to line up the zero with the edge of something to measure.
    - Use a finger to practice measuring something to the quarter inch. (Just move your finger some to make it end at a quarter inch.)
- Day 147 worksheet
- Day 146+ worksheet – Do the next line on the page.

Day 148 (ruler)
- Students will: use a ruler to measure inches, practice facts
- Your child will measure from circle to circle and add together the total number of inches. Have your child say the total after each measurement.
- Day 148 worksheet
- Day 146+ worksheet – Do the next line on the page.

Day 149
- Students will: read Fahrenheit and Celsius thermometers, practice facts
- Day 149 worksheet
    - I think you should do this together and use it as the lesson.
    - Show your child the F next to the thermometers along the top of the page. That means the temperatures shown there are measured in Fahrenheit.
        - Fahrenheit is the last name of the scientist who made the scale. It's how we measure temperature in America.
        - Water freezes at 32 degrees Fahrenheit and boils at 212 degrees.
    - Help your child read the temperatures on the thermometers. The last two have a line halfway between the labeled ten marks. That marks 5 degrees. They will need to count by five to read a temperature that stops at the midway point.
    - Show your child the thermometers with a C next to them. This temperature scale is named for a man with the last name Celsius.
        - This is the temperature scale we use in science and which is used around the world.
        - Here's why it's most popular. On the Celsius scale, water freezes at 0 degrees and boils at 100 degrees.
    - Read the Celsius thermometers together. The last ones have a line for every degree. Count by ones to where the thermometer shows the temperature.
- Day 146+ worksheet – Do the next line on the worksheet.

Day 150
- Students will: estimate temperatures, practice facts
- Day 150 worksheet
  - Make sure your child gets the top correct. Then encourage them to use those numbers to make educated guesses for the rest of the answers. What makes sense?
- Day 146+ worksheet – Do the last line on the page.

Review

Day 151
- Students will: review bar graphs, practice facts
- Day 151 worksheet
- Day 151+ worksheet – Do the first line on the page.

Day 152 (brown crayon)
- Students will: review coins and counting the value of a group of coins, practice facts
- Day 152 worksheet
- Day 151+ worksheet – Do the next line on the page.

Day 153
- Students will: review time and measurement, practice facts
- Day 153 worksheet
- Day 151+ worksheet – Do the next line on the page.

Day 154
- Students will: estimate weights with pounds and ounces, practice facts
- Day 154 worksheet
  - Open the workbook with your child and read the top of the page together. In America we use pounds and ounces when we weigh things. Read the objects and their weights. Tell your child how much they weighed when they were born.
  - They should use the facts at the top of the page to make educated guesses for about how much the items would weigh. They don't need to know how much they weigh, just which answer makes more sense.
- Day 151+ worksheet – Do the next line on the page.

Day 155
- Students will: review addition, subtraction, estimation, counting by tens, using a hundreds chart, word problems
- Day 155 worksheet
  - For Part B help them see that it's three different pieces of the hundreds chart. Can they fill in the blanks? They can look back to Day 92 for help.
- Day 151+ worksheet – Do the last line on the page.

Day 156
- Students will: practice critical thinking skills
- Day 156 worksheet
  - Encourage your child to tackle the activities with a positive attitude. They can do it!
  - The last one doesn't have one set answer. There could be different numbers of goats, dogs, and pigs. There needs to be an odd number of chickens for it to work out.
    - They could use tally marks to keep track of the number of legs as they add animals.

Place Value/Adding Tens and Ones

Day 157
- Students will: review tens and ones
- If you have your tens and ones blocks, you could make numbers with them again.
- Day 157 worksheet
  - Ask your child how many blocks are in each tower.
    - They will count by tens when they count the towers and then count on ones.
- If your child doesn't know their facts yet, please keep working on them.

Day 158
- Students will: combine tens and ones to make numbers
- Day 158 worksheet

Day 159
- Students will: identify the value of digits in numbers up to one hundred
- Day 159 worksheet
  - Turn with your child and look at the first one. Can your child identify which digit is tens and which digit is ones?
  - Have your child read the number out loud, 64, sixty-four.
    - The six isn't six; it's sixty. Sixty is six tens.
  - Encourage your child to read the numbers in Part B out loud to make sure they are sure of the value of each digit.

Day 160
- Students will: write numbers in expanded notation
- If you have your tens and ones blocks, get them out and make numbers. If you don't have your blocks, draw lines for tens and dots for ones.
  - Make a number for your child and then have your child separate it into tens and ones.
  - Write it as an addition problem: tens + ones = total number of blocks.
  - You can hold onto these for Day 174.
- It's called expanded notation to separate a number into its parts, like tens and ones.
  - We write them as addition problems.
- Do it with another number for practice. Separate it into tens and ones and then add them together.
- Day 160 worksheet
  - If your child isn't sure, remind them they can read the number out loud to know the tens value.

Day 161
- Students will: add and subtract tens
- Ask your child what 2 apples plus 3 apples is?
  - 5 apples
- Ask your child what 2 tens plus 3 tens is?
  - 5 tens
- Ask your child what 2 million plus 3 million is?
  - 5 million
- Ask your child what 8 apples minus 5 apples is?
  - 3 apples
- Ask your child what 8 tens minus 5 tens is?
  - 3 tens
- You can ask millions and billions if it makes your child happy. ☺
- On their worksheet they will be adding and subtracting tens.
- Day 161 worksheet

Day 162
- Students will: add and subtract tens in vertical problems
- Day 162 worksheet
  - Look at the worksheet together with your child. Look at the first example together.
  - You can also show your child how they can add straight down, adding the tens together and adding the ones together, which in this case will be zero.

Day 163
- Students will: add and subtract tens in vertical problems
- Day 163 worksheet

Day 164
- Students will: add and subtract tens in vertical problems
- Day 164 worksheet

Day 165
- Students will: add and subtract tens in vertical problems
- Day 165 worksheet
  - This has one trickier one. 50 + 50 will be 10 tens or 100.
  - If they are stuck on it, remind them to add straight down, adding the tens and adding the ones.

Day 166
- Students will: add tens with uneven numbers
- Turn to the Day 92 page in the workbook.
  - Have your child figure out 14 + 10, 14 + 20, 14 + 30.
  - What stays the same and what's different when you add just tens?
    - The tens digit changes and the ones digit stays the same.
    - When you are adding ten, twenty, thirty, etc., how many ones are you adding?
      - zero
      - What's zero plus a number?
        - the same number
- Day 166 worksheet

Day 167
- Students will: solve for missing numbers, review: patterns, shapes, time, graphs, word problems
- Turn to the Day 58 page and review shape names.
- Day 167 worksheet

Day 168
- Students will: subtract tens
- Go back to the Day 92 page and subtract ten from different numbers.
  - What's 78 – 10?
    - What stays the same and what's different?
      - the tens change and the ones stay the same
  - What's 40 – 20?
    - Take away two tens. 4 – 2 = 2
    - The ones are just 0 – 0 which equals 0.
- Day 168 worksheet

Day 169
- Students will: add tens over 100
- Ask your child what 50 + 50 is or 5 tens plus 5 tens.
  - 10 tens or 100, just ten with a zero in the ones place
- Today they'll be adding over 100. You can practice with similar numbers.
  - What's 6 tens plus 8 tens? Remember that it's just like adding 6 apples and 8 apples.
  - 14 tens or fourteen with a zero in the ones place, 140
- Practice until they are comfortable.
- Day 169 worksheet

Day 170
- Students will: subtract tens over 100
- Today you are going to do the same thing with subtraction.
- The ones will just be zero for now. Then they will subtract the tens just like a regular number.
  - Ask your child 12 – 3.
    - 9
  - Now ask 12 tens – 3 tens.
    - 9 tens
  - What number is 9 tens?
    - 90
  - What's 120 – 30?
    - 90
- Day 170 worksheet

Day 171
- Students will: subtract tens and ones without regrouping
- Day 171 worksheet
  - Have your child do the first two problems with pictures. They can cross off tens and ones to visualize subtracting.
  - For Part B show your child how they can subtract the tens and ones straight up and down. Subtract the ones and subtract the tens each by themselves.
  - If there is only one digit, there are no tens to subtract. It's like having a zero for the tens number. Here's an example.
    - 26 – 3 =
      - ones: 6 – 3 = 3
      - tens: 2 – nothing = 2

Day 172
- Students will: add tens and ones without regrouping
- This is the same with addition.
    o They will add the tens and ones separately. They can just do the problems vertically and add the ones and add the tens separately.
    o Where there is no tens digit, they are just adding nothing to the tens, so the tens stay the same.
- Here are two examples to work through.
    o 24 + 35 =
        - ones: 4 + 5 = 9
        - tens: 2 + 3 = 5
    o 31 + 4 =
        - ones: 1 + 4 = 5
        - tens: 3 + nothing = 3

Day 173
- Students will: add and subtract one and two digit numbers from two digit numbers without regrouping
- Day 173 worksheet
    o Warn your child to pay attention if it's asking them to add or subtract!

Day 174
- Students will: add with regrouping
- Ask your child what 6 ones plus 8 ones is.
    o 14 ones
    o What's that in tens and ones?
        - 1 ten and 4 ones
        - The ones turned into a group of ten with some ones left over.
- You could get out your tens and ones blocks or some blocks that you can build towers of ten with or draw pictures.
    o What would 16 plus 8 be?
        - Use blocks or pictures.
            • 24
            • It's ten plus the fourteen ones.
- Day 174 worksheet
    o Have your child color in ten individual blocks.
        - That's a group of ten and will get counted with the groups of ten.
        - The uncolored blocks are the ones in the answer.
    o Show your child how to add vertically using the example.
        - 4 + 8 equals 12.
        - What's 12 in tens and ones?
            • 10 + 2, 1 ten and 2 ones
        - They will write the 2 in the ones spot and the 1 in the tens column to add together with the tens.
    o Stay with your child to encourage them through the problems.

Day 175
- Students will: add two digits with regrouping
- Day 175 worksheet
  - This is more practice with carrying a one to the tens column.

Day 176
- Students will: add two digits with regrouping
- Day 176 worksheet
  - This is more practice with carrying a one to the tens column.

Day 177
- Students will: add two digits with regrouping, solve word problems
- Day 177 worksheet
  - Encourage your child to write the numbers into vertical problems to help them solve the problems.

Day 178
- Students will: add two digit numbers with regrouping
- Day 178 worksheet

Day 179
- Students will: solve word problems with subtraction
- Day 179 worksheet

Day 180
- Students will: use critical thinking skills, finish 2nd grade math!
- Day 180 worksheet
- Celebrate!

EP Math 2

Workbook Answers

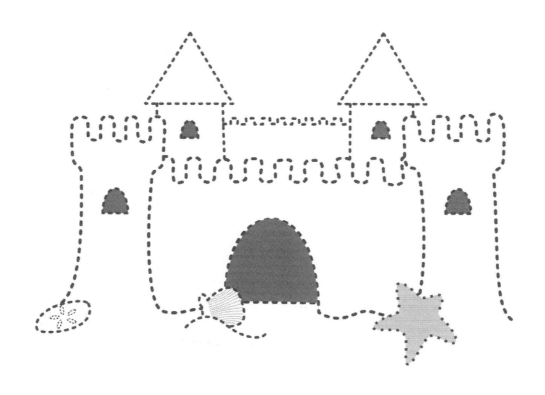

Day 1

Addition & Money

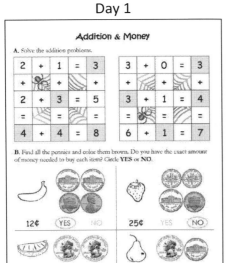

A. Solve the addition problems.

2	+	1	=	3
+		+		+
2	+	3	=	5
=		=		=
4	+	4	=	8

3	+	0	=	3
+		+		+
2	+	1	=	4
=		=		=
6	+	1	=	7

B. Find all the pennies and color them brown. Do you have the exact amount of money needed to buy each item? Circle **YES** or **NO**.

12¢ YES NO
25¢ YES NO
55¢ YES NO
30¢ YES NO

Day 2

Subtraction & Graphing

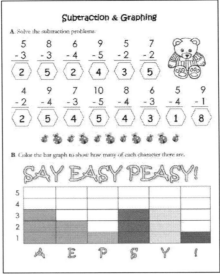

A. Solve the subtraction problems.

5	8	6	9	5	7
-3	-3	-4	-5	-2	-2
2	5	2	4	3	5

4	9	7	10	8	6	5	9
-2	-4	-3	-5	-4	-3	-4	-1
2	5	4	5	4	3	1	8

B. Color the bar graph to show how many of each character there are.

SAY EASY PEASY!

5						
4						
3						
2						
1						
	A	E	P	S	Y	!

Day 3

Addition & Fractions

A. Count and write the number of dots on each dice. Add the numbers.

2 + 3 + 4 + 1 = 10
4 + 2 + 2 + 1 = 9
1 + 3 + 4 = 8

B. Circle the correct fraction of the shaded area.

1/4 2/4 3/4   1/2 1/3 1/4
1/3 2/3 3/3   2/4 2/5 2/6
1/6 3/6 5/6   4/4 4/6 4/8

Day 4

Subtraction & Time

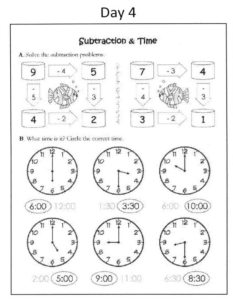

A. Solve the subtraction problems.

9 - 4 = 5
5 - ...
4 - 2 = 2
3 - 2 = 1

7 - 3 = 4

B. What time is it? Circle the correct time.

6:00 12:00
1:30 3:30
6:00 10:00
2:00 5:00
9:00 11:00
6:30 8:30

Day 5

Addition & Subtraction

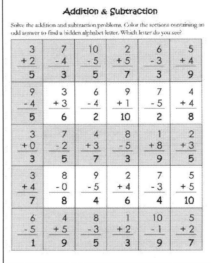

Solve the addition and subtraction problems. Color the sections containing an odd answer to find a hidden alphabet letter. Which letter do you see?

3 +2 5	7 -4 3	10 -5 5	6 +5 7...	6 -3 3	5 +4 9
9 -4 5	3 +3 6	6 -4 2	9 +1 10	7 -5 2	4 +4 8
3 +0 3	7 -2 5	4 +3 7	8 -5 3	1 +8 9	3 +3 5...
3 +4 7	8 -0 8	9 -5 4	2 +4 6	7 -3 4	5 +5 10
6 -5 1	4 +5 9	8 -3 5	1 +2 3	10 -1 9	5 +2 7

Day 6+

My 201-300 Chart

From **Day 6** to **Day 10**, use this chart to practice counting from 201 to 300.

201	202	203							210
211	212	213							220
221	222	223							230
231	232	233							240
241	242	243							250
251	252	253							260
261	262	263							270
271	272	273							280
281	282	283							290
291	292	293							300

- On **Day 6**, write 201 in the first corner square. Fill in the 1s column. The next number is 211. The last number should be 291.
- On **Day 7**, fill in the 2s column. Write 202 next to 201 and then fill in the rest of the column. The last number should be 292.
- On **Day 8**, fill in the 3s column. The last number should be 293.
- On **Day 10**, fill in the 10s column. The last number should be 300.

Day 6

Counting to 100

Color in the 1s column. Color 1, then 11, then 21, all the way down to 91.

1	2	3	4	5	6	7	8	9	10
11	12	13	14	15	16	17	18	19	20
21	22	23	24	25	26	27	28	29	30
31	32	33	34	35	36	37	38	39	40
41	42	43	44	45	46	47	48	49	50
51	52	53	54	55	56	57	58	59	60
61	62	63	64	65	66	67	68	69	70
71	72	73	84	75	76	77	78	79	80
81	82	83	84	85	86	87	88	89	90
91	92	93	94	95	96	97	98	99	100

Day 7

Counting by 2s

A. Count by 2s out loud and fill in the missing numbers.

4 6 8 10 12 14 16 18
50 52 54 56 58 60 62 64
76 78 80 82 84 86 88 90

B. Help the bee find the flower. Count by 2s. Color the squares as you count.

20	22	24	16	72	74	76	78	80
32	30	28	26	84	70	18	42	66	82
34	43	38	48	76	68	26	88	86	84
36	22	48	50	52	66	64	90	92	76
38	52	46	64	54	20	62	46	94	42
40	42	44	62	56	58	60	74		

Finish

Day 8

Counting by 3s

A. Count by 3s. Connect the dots from 3 to 99 to complete the drawing.

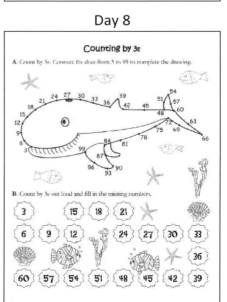

B. Count by 3s out loud and fill in the missing numbers.

3 15 18 21
6 9 12 24 27 30 33
36
60 57 54 51 48 45 42 39

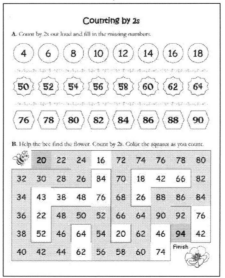
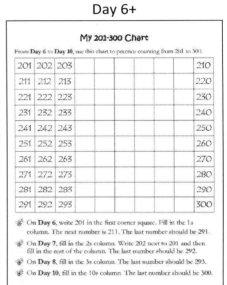

Day 9

Counting by 5s

A. Count by 5s. Connect the dots from 5 to 60 to complete the drawing.

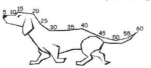

B. Color in as you count by 5s. Start by coloring in 185 and 190.

181	182	183	184	185	186	187	188	189	190
191	192	193	194	195	196	197	198	199	200
201	202	203	204	205	206	207	208	209	210
211	212	213	214	215	216	217	218	219	220
221	222	223	224	225	226	227	228	229	230
231	232	233	234	235	236	237	238	239	240
241	242	243	244	245	246	247	248	249	250
251	252	253	254	255	256	257	258	259	260
261	262	263	264	265	266	267	268	269	270
271	272	273	274	275	276	277	278	279	280

Day 10

Counting by 10s

A. Count by 10s out loud and fill in the missing numbers.

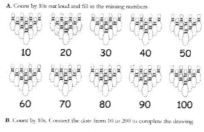

10	20	30	40	50
60	70	80	90	100

B. Count by 10s. Connect the dots from 10 to 200 to complete the drawing.

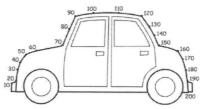

Day 11+

My Facts List I

From **Day 11** to **Day 50**, use these worksheets to write down new math facts you learn. You can use them to review and practice.

6 + 2 = 8		6 + 3 = 9
2 + 6 = 8		3 + 6 = 9
6 + 4 = 10		6 + 5 = 11
4 + 6 = 10		5 + 6 = 11
6 + 6 = 12		7 + 2 = 9
+ =		2 + 7 = 9
7 + 3 = 10		7 + 4 = 11
3 + 7 = 10		4 + 7 = 11

Day 11+

My Facts List II

From **Day 11** to **Day 50**, use these worksheets to write down new math facts you learn. You can use them to review and practice.

7 + 5 = 12		7 + 6 = 13
5 + 7 = 12		6 + 7 = 13
7 + 7 = 14		8 + 8 = 16
+ =		
9 + 9 = 18		8 + 2 = 10
		2 + 8 = 10
		8 + 3 = 11
		3 + 8 = 11
		8 + 4 = 12
		4 + 8 = 12

Day 11+

My Facts List III

From **Day 11** to **Day 50**, use these worksheets to write down new math facts you learn. You can use them to review and practice.

8 + 5 = 13		8 + 6 = 14
5 + 8 = 13		6 + 8 = 14
8 + 7 = 15		9 + 2 = 11
7 + 8 = 15		2 + 9 = 11
9 + 3 = 12		9 + 4 = 13
3 + 9 = 12		4 + 9 = 13
9 + 5 = 14		9 + 6 = 15
5 + 9 = 14		6 + 9 = 15
9 + 7 = 16		9 + 8 = 17
7 + 9 = 16		8 + 9 = 17

Day 11

Addition up to 6 + 2

A. Practice addition up to 6 + 2.

6	4	5	3	4	5	3	6
+2	+2	+2	+2	+2	+2	+2	+2
8	6	7	5	6	7	5	8

B. Practice addition up to 2 + 6.

2	2	2	2	2	2	2	2
+6	+4	+3	+2	+5	+6	+3	+6
8	6	5	4	7	8	5	8

C. Let's count by 1s! Find a path along the answers in order from 1 to 10.

4 - 3	2 + 5	3 + 4	2 + 6
6 - 4	8 - 5	7 - 1	4 + 5
5 - 3	7 - 3	9 - 4	10 - 0

Day 12

Addition up to 6 + 3

A. Practice addition up to 6 + 3.

6	4	5	4	3	6	6	5
+3	+2	+2	+3	+2	+2	+3	+3
9	6	7	7	5	8	9	8

B. Practice addition up to 3 + 6.

3	3	3	3	3	3	2	2
+6	+5	+3	+4	+4	+6	+5	+6
9	8	6	7	7	9	7	8

C. Connect the addition problems to their correct answers.

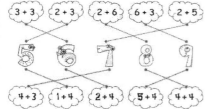

Day 13

Addition up to 6 + 4

A. Practice addition up to 6 + 4.

6	4	5	2	3	6	4	6
+4	+3	+4	+3	+4	+2	+3	+4
10	8	6	9	7	8	7	10

B. Practice addition up to 4 + 6.

4	2	3	4	3	4	4	3
+6	+5	+3	+4	+5	+6	+5	+6
10	7	6	8	8	10	9	9

C. Connect the subtraction problems to their correct answers.

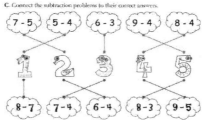

Day 14

Counting to 500

A. Count by 10s. Connect the dots from 100 to 500 to complete the drawing.

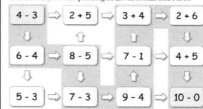

B. Compare the numbers with < (less than), > (greater than), or = (equal to).

3 < 6	18 > 11	8 < 18
4 > 2	10 < 12	14 > 6
9 > 7	15 < 19	17 < 19
8 = 8	20 = 20	16 > 5
1 < 5	14 > 13	12 = 12

Day 15

Comparing Numbers

A. Compare the numbers with < (less than), > (greater than), or = (equal to).

95 > 45	242 < 532	345 < 354
38 > 26	321 < 881	88 < 216
72 = 72	285 > 149	72 < 824
88 < 95	626 = 626	935 > 56
50 < 53	967 > 427	624 > 100

B. Compare the sums with < (less than), > (greater than), or = (equal to).

6 + 4 = 5 + 5	3 + 3 < 2 + 6
3 + 6 > 2 + 5	2 + 4 < 4 + 4
5 + 3 > 3 + 4	3 + 6 = 4 + 5
3 + 5 < 4 + 5	4 + 6 > 5 + 2
1 + 7 < 6 + 3	2 + 5 = 4 + 3

Day 16

Addition up to 6 + 5

A. Practice addition up to 6 + 5.

6 +5 = 11	5 +2 = 7	5 +4 = 9	6 +3 = 9	5 +3 = 8	4 +3 = 7	6 +4 = 10	6 +5 = 11

B. Practice addition up to 5 + 6.

5 +6 = 11	4 +5 = 9	5 +5 = 8	5 +6 = 11	5 +5 = 10	4 +6 = 10	4 +4 = 8	5 +4 = 9

C. Solve the subtraction problems.

9 − 5 = 4	4 − 2 = 2	6 − 3 = 3	10 − 5 = 5
7 − 5 = 2	5 − 2 = 3	3 − 3 = 0	8 − 5 = 3

D. Count by 2s from 22 to 100.

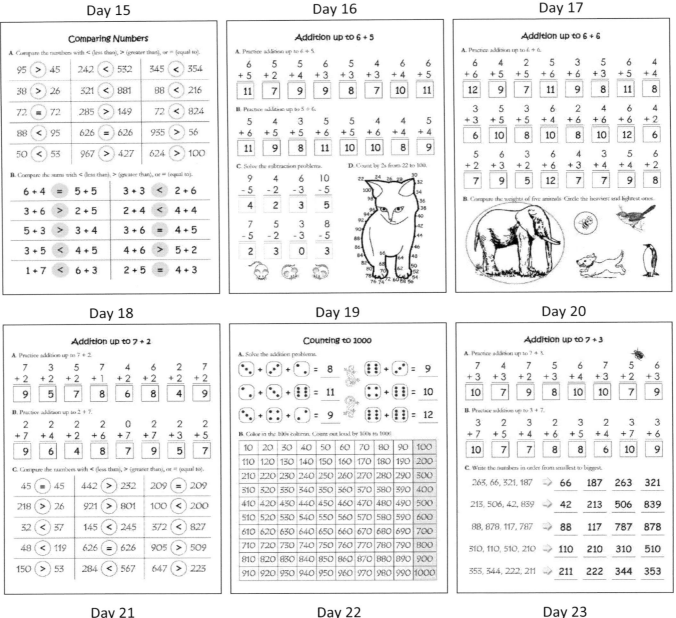

Day 17

Addition up to 6 + 6

A. Practice addition up to 6 + 6.

6 +6 = 12	4 +5 = 9	2 +5 = 7	5 +6 = 11	3 +6 = 9	5 +3 = 8	6 +5 = 11	4 +4 = 8
3 +3 = 6	5 +5 = 10	3 +5 = 8	6 +4 = 10	2 +6 = 8	4 +6 = 10	6 +6 = 12	4 +2 = 6
5 +2 = 7	3 +3 = 9	6 +2 = 5	3 +6 = 12	4 +3 = 7	3 +4 = 7	5 +4 = 9	6 +2 = 8

B. Compare the weights of five animals. Circle the heaviest and lightest ones.

Day 18

Addition up to 7 + 2

A. Practice addition up to 7 + 2.

7 +2 = 9	3 +2 = 5	5 +2 = 7	4 +1 = 8	6 +2 = 8	2 +2 = 4	2 +2 = 4	7 +2 = 9

B. Practice addition up to 2 + 7.

2 +7 = 9	2 +4 = 6	2 +2 = 4	2 +6 = 8	2 +7 = 9	2 +7 = 7	2 +3 = 5	2 +5 = 7

C. Compare the numbers with < (less than), > (greater than), or = (equal to).

45 = 45	442 > 232	209 = 209
218 > 26	921 > 801	100 < 200
32 < 37	145 < 245	372 < 827
48 < 119	626 = 626	905 > 509
150 > 53	284 < 567	647 > 223

Day 19

Counting to 1000

A. Solve the addition problems.

⚀ + ⚁ + ⚀ = 8   ⚃ + ⚄ = 9
⚀ + ⚁ + ⚅ = 11   ⚄ + ⚄ = 10
⚀ + ⚄ + ⚀ = 9   ⚅ + ⚅ = 12

B. Color in the 100s column. Count out loud by 100s to 1000.

10	20	30	40	50	60	70	80	90	100
110	120	130	140	150	160	170	180	190	200
210	220	230	240	250	260	270	280	290	300
310	320	330	340	350	360	370	380	390	400
410	420	430	440	450	460	470	480	490	500
510	520	530	540	550	560	570	580	590	600
610	620	630	640	650	660	670	680	690	700
710	720	730	740	750	760	770	780	790	800
810	820	830	840	850	860	870	880	890	900
910	920	930	940	950	960	970	980	990	1000

Day 20

Addition up to 7 + 3

A. Practice addition up to 7 + 3.

7 +3 = 10	4 +3 = 7	7 +2 = 9	5 +3 = 8	7 +3 = 10	7 +3 = 10	5 +2 = 7	6 +3 = 9

B. Practice addition up to 3 + 7.

3 +7 = 10	2 +5 = 7	3 +4 = 8	2 +6 = 8	3 +5 = 8	2 +4 = 6	3 +7 = 10	3 +6 = 9

C. Write the numbers in order from smallest to biggest.

263, 66, 321, 187 ⇒	66	187	263	321
213, 506, 42, 839 ⇒	42	213	506	839
88, 878, 117, 787 ⇒	88	117	787	878
310, 110, 510, 210 ⇒	110	210	310	510
353, 344, 222, 211 ⇒	211	222	344	353

Day 21

Addition & Skip Counting

A. Practice addition up to 7 + 3 and 3 + 7.

6 +6 = 12	6 +4 = 10	2 +7 = 9	5 +6 = 11	6 +3 = 9	3 +7 = 10	2 +6 = 8	5 +5 = 10
6 +5 = 11	7 +3 = 10	6 +2 = 8	4 +4 = 8	7 +2 = 9	4 +6 = 10	5 +4 = 9	3 +6 = 9

B. Find three paths to the cheese. Count by 1s from 1 to 10, by 10s from 10 to 100 and by 100s from 100 to 1000. Color each path using different colors.

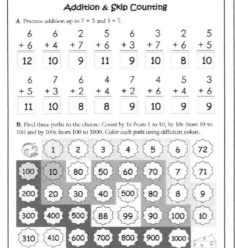

Day 22

Addition up to 7 + 4

A. Practice addition up to 7 + 4.

7 +4 = 11	6 +2 = 8	3 +3 = 6	4 +4 = 8	6 +3 = 9	3 +2 = 5	5 +4 = 9	7 +4 = 11
6 +3 = 10	4 +2 = 6	5 +3 = 8	7 +4 = 11	5 +2 = 7	3 +4 = 9	6 +4 = 10	4 +3 = 11

B. Practice addition up to 4 + 7.

4 +7 = 11	2 +5 = 8	3 +6 = 9	2 +6 = 8	3 +5 = 9	4 +7 = 11	3 +6 = 9	4 +7 = 11

C. Draw a circle around each odd number.

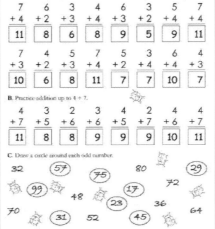

32, (57), (75), 80, (29), (99), 48, (17), 72, 70, (23), 36, 64, (31), 52, (45)

Day 23

Addition up to 7 + 5

A. Practice addition up to 7 + 5.

7 +5 = 12	6 +4 = 10	4 +3 = 7	3 +5 = 8	7 +4 = 11	6 +2 = 8	7 +5 = 12	4 +4 = 8
5 +5 = 10	5 +5 = 10	3 +6 = 9	6 +6 = 12	5 +4 = 9	5 +2 = 7	5 +2 = 7	6 +5 = 11

B. Practice addition up to 5 + 7.

5 +7 = 12	2 +6 = 8	3 +6 = 9	5 +7 = 12	4 +6 = 10	2 +7 = 9	4 +6 = 11	4 +7 = 11

C. Solve the subtraction problems.

9 −4 → 5 −5 → 4   8 −5 → 3 −2 → 1

Day 24

Addition up to 7 + 6

A. Practice addition up to 7 + 6.

$7+6=13$	$4+6=10$	$6+6=12$	$5+4=9$	$6+4=10$	$7+2=9$	$5+5=10$	$7+5=12$
$6+5=11$	$7+6=13$	$6+3=9$	$7+4=11$	$4+5=9$	$6+2=8$	$7+6=13$	$5+6=11$

B. Practice addition up to 6 + 7.

$6+7=13$	$5+3=8$	$3+7=10$	$5+5=10$	$5+7=12$	$3+6=9$	$4+7=11$	$6+7=13$

C. Color the rectangles containing an even number to find a hidden word.

10	69	22	13	98	56	82	49	20	74	94
36	63	39	77	16	87	65	15	88	51	99
98	40	16	53	82	66	50	67	58	60	86
37	75	84	55	30	29	89	25	44	79	41
76	52	38	27	78	54	92	43	80	32	100

Day 25

Doubles Facts

A. Practice doubles facts up to 9 + 9.

$2+2=4$	$3+3=6$	$4+4=8$	$5+5=10$	$6+6=12$	$7+7=14$	$8+8=16$	$9+9=18$

B. Practice doubles facts up to 9 + 9. Fill in the blanks.

Double 2 = 4   Double 6 = 12
Double 9 = 18   Double 3 = 6
Double 8 = 16   Double 7 = 14
Double 4 = 8   Double 5 = 10

C. Solve the addition and subtraction problems.

8	−	4	=	4		4	+	3	=	7
−				+		+				
5	−	3	=	2		5	−	2	=	3
=				=		=				
3		3	+	6	=	9		1		4

Day 26

Addition up to 7 + 7

A. Practice addition up to 7 + 7.

$4+6=10$	$5+5=10$	$3+7=10$	$5+6=11$	$7+7=14$	$5+2=7$	$2+6=8$	$7+5=12$
$4+7=11$	$6+6=12$	$5+4=9$	$4+3=13$	$6+5=8$	$6+7=14$	$5+3$	$7+7$

B. Solve the addition problems.

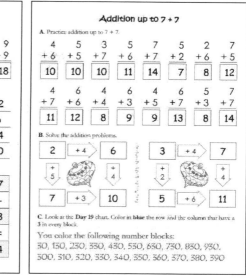

2 [+4] 6   3 [+4] 7
[+5]   [+2]
7 [+3] 10   5 [+6] 11

C. Look at the Day 19 chart. Color in blue the row and the column that have a 3 in every block.

You color the following number blocks:
30, 130, 230, 330, 430, 530, 630, 730, 830, 930,
300, 310, 320, 330, 340, 350, 360, 370, 380, 390

Day 27

Addition up to 8 + 2

A. Practice addition up to 8 + 2.

$8+2=10$	$5+2=7$	$3+2=5$	$6+2=8$	$4+2=6$	$7+2=9$	$2+2=4$	$8+2=10$

B. Practice addition up to 2 + 8.

$2+8=10$	$2+6=8$	$2+7=9$	$2+5=7$	$2+3=5$	$2+4=6$	$2+8=10$	$2+7=9$

C. Match each number word to the number.

Six hundred twenty • • 839
Two hundred fifteen • • 782
Four hundred forty-five • • 620
Nine hundred sixty-three • • 328
Eight hundred thirty-nine • • 215
Seven hundred eighty-two • • 963
Three hundred twenty-eight • • 445

Day 28

Addition up to 8 + 3

A. Practice addition up to 8 + 3.

$8+3=11$	$5+3=8$	$7+2=9$	$6+3=9$	$6+2=8$	$8+3=11$	$5+2=7$	$7+3=10$

B. Practice addition up to 3 + 8.

$3+8=11$	$2+5=7$	$2+7=9$	$3+6=9$	$2+8=10$	$2+6=8$	$3+7=10$	$3+8=11$

C. Circle the number that comes before and after.

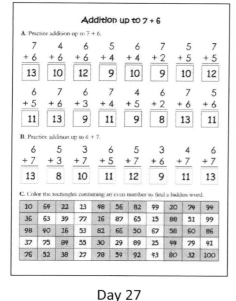

BEFORE (41) — [42] — AFTER (43)   BEFORE (35) — [36] — AFTER (37)
BEFORE (70) — [71] — (72)   BEFORE (64) — [65] — (66)
BEFORE (89) — [90] — (91)   BEFORE (22) — [23] — (24)

Day 29

Addition up to 8 + 4

A. Practice addition up to 8 + 4.

$8+4=12$	$5+3=8$	$7+4=11$	$4+2=6$	$6+4=10$	$4+4=8$	$8+4=12$	$6+2=8$
$7+2=9$	$6+3=9$	$4+3=7$	$5+2=7$	$8+4=12$	$5+4=9$	$3+4=7$	$7+3=10$

B. Practice addition up to 4 + 8.

$4+8=12$	$2+8=10$	$3+7=10$	$4+6=10$	$2+7=9$	$3+6=9$	$4+8=12$	$3+8=11$

C. Circle the number that comes before and after.

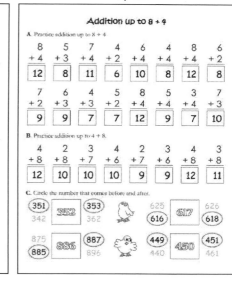

(351) — [352] — (353)   (616) — [617] — (618)
(885) — [886] — (887)   (449) — [450] — (451)

Day 30

Addition & Comparison

A. Connect the problems to their correct answers.

6 + 5		3 + 6
2 + 7	8	4 + 7
6 + 6	9	6 + 2
4 + 4	10	5 + 7
3 + 7	11, 12	4 + 6

B. Compare the numbers with < (less than), > (greater than), or = (equal to).

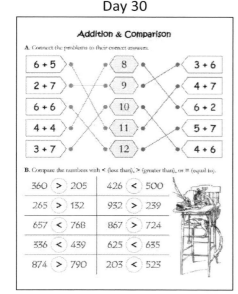

360 > 205	426 < 500
265 > 132	932 > 239
657 < 768	867 > 724
336 < 439	625 < 635
874 > 790	203 < 523

Day 31

Addition & Subtraction

A. Solve the addition problems.

$7+7=14$	$6+5=11$	$3+8=11$	$7+3=10$	$6+6=12$	$7+6=13$	$4+5=9$	$8+2=10$
$5+7=12$	$4+5=9$	$6+5=11$	$4+6=10$	$7+3=10$	$6+4=10$	$5+5=10$	$4+8=12$

B. Solve the addition and subtraction problems.

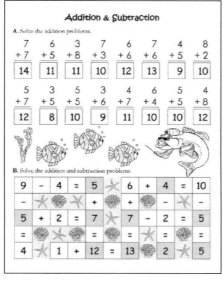

9	−	4	=	5		6	+	4	=	10
−				+		+				−
5	+	2	=	7		7	−	2	=	5
=				=		=				=
4		1	+	12	=	13		2		5

Day 32

Addition up to 8 + 5

A. Practice addition up to 8 + 5.

$8+5=13$	$5+4=9$	$6+5=11$	$7+3=10$	$4+5=9$	$7+4=11$	$4+4=8$	$8+3=11$
$6+4=10$	$4+5=8$	$8+5=13$	$4+3=7$	$5+5=10$	$6+3=8$	$3+5=8$	$6+3=9$

B. Practice addition up to 5 + 8.

$5+8=13$	$4+6=10$	$5+4=9$	$4+8=12$	$5+8=13$	$4+7=11$	$3+8=11$	$5+7=12$

C. Count by 5s. Fill in the missing numbers to complete the sequence.

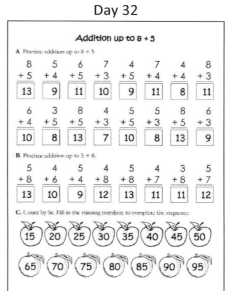

15 · 20 · 25 · 30 · 35 · 40 · 45 · 50
65 · 70 · 75 · 80 · 85 · 90 · 95

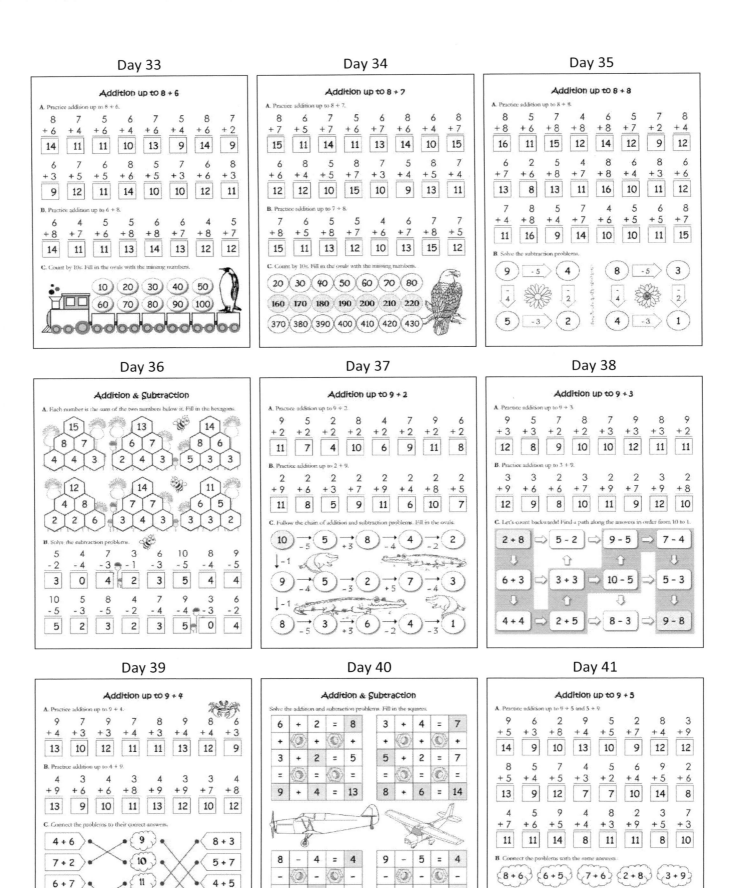

Day 33
Addition up to 8 + 6

A. Practice addition up to 8 + 6.

8	7	5	6	7	5	8	7
+6	+4	+6	+4	+6	+4	+6	+2
14	11	11	10	13	9	14	9

6	7	6	8	5	7	6	8
+3	+5	+5	+6	+5	+3	+6	+3
9	12	11	14	10	10	12	11

B. Practice addition up to 6 + 8.

6	4	5	6	6	6	4	5
+8	+7	+6	+8	+8	+7	+8	+7
14	11	11	13	14	13	12	12

C. Count by 10s. Fill in the ovals with the missing numbers.

10 20 30 40 50 60 70 80 90 100

Day 34
Addition up to 8 + 7

A. Practice addition up to 8 + 7.

8	6	7	5	6	8	6	8
+7	+5	+7	+6	+7	+6	+4	+7
15	11	14	11	13	14	10	15

6	8	5	8	6	5	8	7
+6	+4	+5	+7	+3	+4	+5	+4
12	12	10	15	9	9	13	11

B. Practice addition up to 7 + 8.

7	6	6	6	7	6	7	7
+8	+5	+8	+7	+6	+7	+8	+5
15	11	14	13	13	13	15	12

C. Count by 10s. Fill in the ovals with the missing numbers.

20 30 40 50 60 70 80
160 170 180 190 200 210 220
370 380 390 400 410 420 430

Day 35
Addition up to 8 + 8

A. Practice addition up to 8 + 8.

8	6	7	4	6	5	7	8
+8	+6	+8	+8	+8	+7	+2	+4
16	11	15	12	14	12	9	12

6	2	5	4	8	6	8	6
+7	+6	+8	+7	+8	+4	+3	+6
13	8	13	11	16	10	11	12

7	8	5	7	4	9	5	8
+4	+8	+4	+7	+6	+5	+5	+7
11	16	9	14	10	14	10	15

B. Solve the subtraction problems.

9 − 5 → 4   8 − 5 → 3
− 4   − 2
5 − 3 → 2   4 − 3 → 1

Day 36
Addition & Subtraction

A. Each number is the sum of the two numbers below it. Fill in the hexagons.

15 / 8 7 / 4 4 3
13 / 6 7 / 3 4 3
14 / 8 6 / 5 3 3

12 / 4 8 / 2 2 6
14 / 7 7 / 3 4 3
11 / 6 5 / 3 3 2

B. Solve the subtraction problems.

5	4	7	3	6	10	8	9
−2	−4	−3	−1	−3	−5	−4	−5
3	0	4	2	3	5	4	4

10	5	8	4	7	9	3	6
−5	−3	−5	−2	−4	−4	−3	−2
5	2	3	2	3	5	0	4

Day 37
Addition up to 9 + 2

A. Practice addition up to 9 + 2.

9	5	2	8	4	7	9	6
+2	+2	+2	+2	+2	+2	+2	+2
11	7	4	10	6	9	11	8

B. Practice addition up to 2 + 9.

2	2	2	2	2	2	2	2
+9	+6	+3	+7	+9	+4	+8	+5
11	8	5	9	11	6	10	7

C. Follow the chain of addition and subtraction problems. Fill in the ovals.

10 −5 → 5 +3 → 8 −4 → 4 −2 → 2
↓ −1
9 −4 → 5 −3 → 2 +5 → 7 −4 → 3
↓ −1
8 −5 → 3 +3 → 6 −2 → 4 −3 → 1

Day 38
Addition up to 9 + 3

A. Practice addition up to 9 + 3.

9	5	7	8	7	9	8	9
+3	+3	+2	+3	+3	+3	+3	+2
12	8	9	10	10	12	11	11

B. Practice addition up to 3 + 9.

3	3	2	3	2	3	2	2
+9	+6	+6	+7	+9	+7	+9	+8
12	9	8	10	11	9	11	10

C. Let's count backwards! Find a path along the answers in order from 10 to 1.

2+8 → 5−2 → 9−5 → 7−4
6+3 → 3+3 → 10−5 → 5−3
4+4 → 2+5 → 8−3 → 9−8

Day 39
Addition up to 9 + 4

A. Practice addition up to 9 + 4.

9	7	9	7	8	9	8	6
+4	+3	+3	+4	+3	+4	+4	+3
13	10	12	11	11	13	12	9

B. Practice addition up to 4 + 9.

4	3	4	3	4	3	3	4
+9	+6	+6	+8	+9	+9	+7	+8
13	9	10	11	13	12	10	12

C. Connect the problems to their correct answers.

4 + 6   9   8 + 3
7 + 2   10   5 + 7
6 + 7   11   4 + 5
6 + 5   12   3 + 7
4 + 8   13   4 + 9

Day 40
Addition & Subtraction

Solve the addition and subtraction problems. Fill in the squares.

6 + 2 = 8
+   +
3 + 2 = 5
=   =
9 + 4 = 13

3 + 4 = 7
+   +
5 + 2 = 7
=   =
8 + 6 = 14

8 − 4 = 4
−   −
3 − 2 = 1
=   =
5 − 2 = 3

9 − 5 = 4
−   −
4 − 3 = 1
=   =
5 − 2 = 3

Day 41
Addition up to 9 + 5

A. Practice addition up to 9 + 5 and 5 + 9.

9	6	2	9	5	2	8	3
+5	+3	+8	+4	+5	+7	+4	+9
14	9	10	13	10	9	12	12

8	5	7	4	5	6	9	2
+5	+4	+5	+3	+2	+4	+5	+6
13	9	12	7	7	10	14	8

4	5	9	4	8	2	3	7
+7	+6	+5	+4	+3	+9	+5	+3
11	11	14	8	11	11	8	10

B. Connect the problems with the same answers.

8 + 6   6 + 5   7 + 6   2 + 8   3 + 9
4 + 7   5 + 5   9 + 5   6 + 6   5 + 8

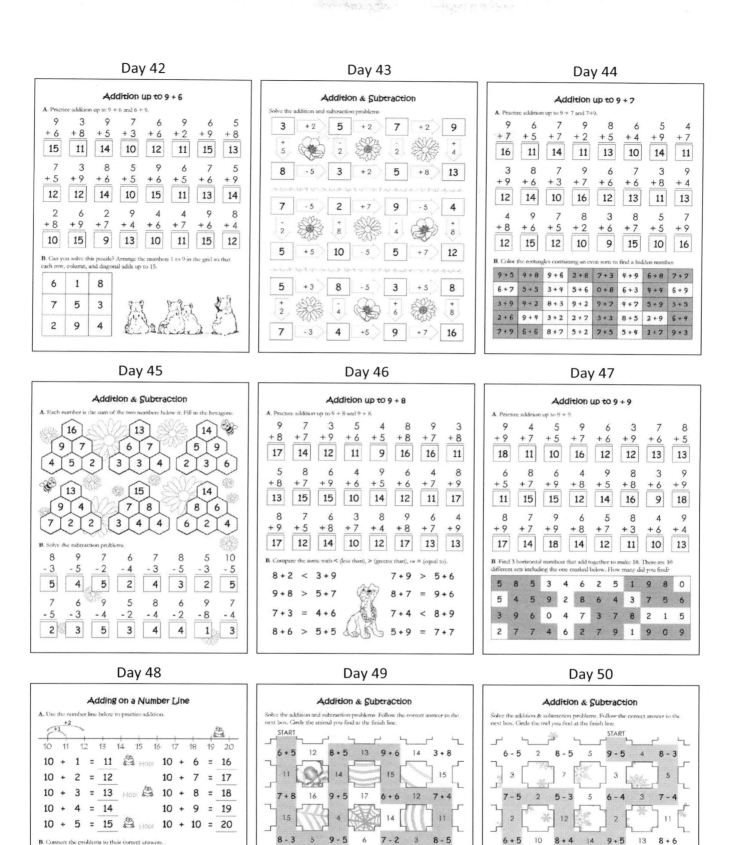

Day 51+

Daily Practice for the Week

From **Day 51** to **Day 55**, solve one row of problems each day.

4 − 2 = 2	8 − 5 = 3	5 − 3 = 2	7 − 4 = 3	3 − 1 = 2	9 − 5 = 4	6 − 2 = 4	10 − 5 = 5
7 + 9 = 16	8 + 6 = 14	9 + 5 = 14	6 + 6 = 12	4 + 9 = 13	7 + 7 = 14	9 + 9 = 18	8 + 7 = 15
7 − 2 = 5	5 − 2 = 3	6 − 3 = 3	8 − 4 = 4	10 − 9 = 1	4 − 2 = 2	7 − 3 = 4	9 − 4 = 5
6 + 5 = 11	6 + 8 = 14	7 + 6 = 13	9 + 8 = 17	7 + 5 = 12	8 + 3 = 11	6 + 9 = 15	5 + 8 = 13
6 − 4 = 2	8 − 5 = 3	7 − 4 = 3	9 − 5 = 4	10 − 5 = 5	7 − 5 = 2	5 − 4 = 1	8 − 3 = 5

Day 51

Tens and Ones

Circle the groups of ten. Count the tens and ones. Write the numbers.

2 tens + 5 ones = 25
2 tens + 3 ones = 23
2 tens + 7 ones = 27
2 tens + 0 ones = 20
3 tens + 6 ones = 36
3 tens + 8 ones = 38

Day 52

Tens and Ones II

Count the number of blocks in each set. Write the numbers.

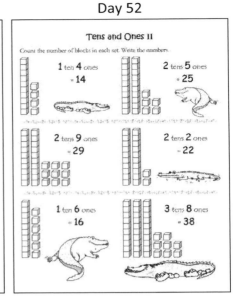

1 ten 4 ones = 14
2 tens 5 ones = 25
2 tens 9 ones = 29
2 tens 2 ones = 22
1 ten 6 ones = 16
3 tens 8 ones = 38

Day 53

Tens and Ones

Write the correct number in each blank.

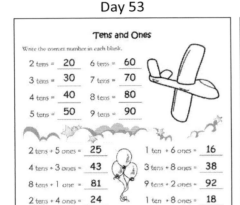

2 tens = 20   6 tens = 60
3 tens = 30   7 tens = 70
4 tens = 40   8 tens = 80
5 tens = 50   9 tens = 90

2 tens + 5 ones = 25   1 ten + 6 ones = 16
4 tens + 3 ones = 43   3 tens + 8 ones = 38
8 tens + 1 one = 81   9 tens + 2 ones = 92
2 tens + 4 ones = 24   1 ten + 8 ones = 18
4 tens + 2 ones = 42   3 tens + 1 one = 31
8 tens + 9 ones = 89   9 tens + 5 ones = 95
5 tens + 8 ones = 58   6 tens + 4 ones = 64
3 tens + 2 ones = 32   7 tens + 3 ones = 73

Day 54

Tens and Ones

Count the number of blocks in each set. Write the numbers.

34   56
29   42
45   60

Day 55

Tens and Ones

Write the correct number of tens and ones for each number.

	TENS	ONES			TENS	ONES
73	7	3		35	3	5
29	2	9		61	6	1
43	4	3		82	8	2
58	5	8		14	1	4
32	3	2		55	5	5
47	4	7		96	9	6

Day 56+

Daily Practice for the Week

From **Day 56** to **Day 60**, solve one row of problems each day.

8 + 4 = 12	9 + 7 = 16	8 + 5 = 13	4 + 7 = 11	7 + 8 = 15	3 + 9 = 12	5 + 7 = 12	8 + 9 = 17
7 − 2 = 5	9 − 5 = 4	6 − 3 = 3	4 − 4 = 1	3 − 1 = 2	10 − 5 = 5	5 − 2 = 3	8 − 3 = 5
5 + 9 = 14	3 + 8 = 11	7 + 4 = 11	4 + 6 = 10	6 + 7 = 13	6 + 3 = 9	9 + 6 = 15	4 + 8 = 12
5 − 3 = 2	10 − 5 = 5	7 − 4 = 3	4 − 2 = 2	9 − 4 = 5	8 − 5 = 3	3 − 2 = 1	6 − 2 = 4
6 − 4 = 2	5 − 2 = 3	9 − 5 = 4	8 − 4 = 4	8 − 3 = 5	4 − 2 = 2	7 − 5 = 2	6 − 3 = 3

Day 56

Tens and Ones

Count the number of blocks in each set. Write the numbers.

21   24   35
23   97
59   78

Day 57

Tens and Ones

Count the number of blocks in each set. Write the numbers.

15   23   34
30   99
58   83

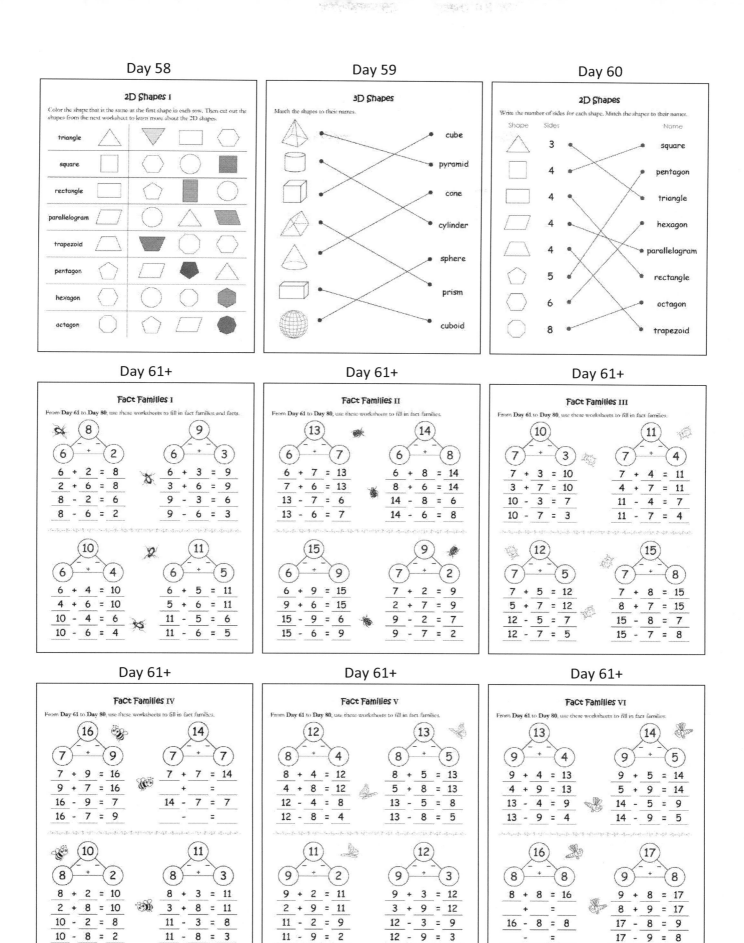

Day 58

2D Shapes I

Color the shape that is the same as the first shape in each row. Then cut out the shapes from the next worksheet to learn more about the 2D shapes.

triangle				
square				
rectangle				
parallelogram				
trapezoid				
pentagon				
hexagon				
octagon				

Day 59

3D Shapes

Match the shapes to their names.

- cube
- pyramid
- cone
- cylinder
- sphere
- prism
- cuboid

Day 60

2D Shapes

Write the number of sides for each shape. Match the shapes to their names.

Shape	Sides		Name
△	3		square
□	4		pentagon
▭	4		triangle
▱	4		hexagon
▱	4		parallelogram
⬠	5		rectangle
⬡	6		octagon
⯃	8		trapezoid

Day 61+

Fact Families I

From **Day 61** to **Day 80**, use these worksheets to fill in fact families and facts.

8 / 6 + 2

6 + 2 = 8
2 + 6 = 8
8 - 2 = 6
8 - 6 = 2

9 / 6 + 3

6 + 3 = 9
3 + 6 = 9
9 - 3 = 6
9 - 6 = 3

10 / 6 + 4

6 + 4 = 10
4 + 6 = 10
10 - 4 = 6
10 - 6 = 4

11 / 6 + 5

6 + 5 = 11
5 + 6 = 11
11 - 5 = 6
11 - 6 = 5

Day 61+

Fact Families II

From **Day 61** to **Day 80**, use these worksheets to fill in fact families.

13 / 6 + 7

6 + 7 = 13
7 + 6 = 13
13 - 7 = 6
13 - 6 = 7

14 / 6 + 8

6 + 8 = 14
8 + 6 = 14
14 - 8 = 6
14 - 6 = 8

15 / 6 + 9

6 + 9 = 15
9 + 6 = 15
15 - 9 = 6
15 - 6 = 9

9 / 7 + 2

7 + 2 = 9
2 + 7 = 9
9 - 2 = 7
9 - 7 = 2

Day 61+

Fact Families III

From **Day 61** to **Day 80**, use these worksheets to fill in fact families.

10 / 7 + 3

7 + 3 = 10
3 + 7 = 10
10 - 3 = 7
10 - 7 = 3

11 / 7 + 4

7 + 4 = 11
4 + 7 = 11
11 - 4 = 7
11 - 7 = 4

12 / 7 + 5

7 + 5 = 12
5 + 7 = 12
12 - 5 = 7
12 - 7 = 5

15 / 7 + 8

7 + 8 = 15
8 + 7 = 15
15 - 8 = 7
15 - 7 = 8

Day 61+

Fact Families IV

From **Day 61** to **Day 80**, use these worksheets to fill in fact families.

16 / 7 + 9

7 + 9 = 16
9 + 7 = 16
16 - 9 = 7
16 - 7 = 9

14 / 7 + 7

7 + 7 = 14
___ + ___ = ___
14 - 7 = 7
___ - ___ = ___

10 / 8 + 2

8 + 2 = 10
2 + 8 = 10
10 - 2 = 8
10 - 8 = 2

11 / 8 + 3

8 + 3 = 11
3 + 8 = 11
11 - 3 = 8
11 - 8 = 3

Day 61+

Fact Families V

From **Day 61** to **Day 80**, use these worksheets to fill in fact families.

12 / 8 + 4

8 + 4 = 12
4 + 8 = 12
12 - 4 = 8
12 - 8 = 4

13 / 8 + 5

8 + 5 = 13
5 + 8 = 13
13 - 5 = 8
13 - 8 = 5

11 / 9 + 2

9 + 2 = 11
2 + 9 = 11
11 - 2 = 9
11 - 9 = 2

12 / 9 + 3

9 + 3 = 12
3 + 9 = 12
12 - 3 = 9
12 - 9 = 3

Day 61+

Fact Families VI

From **Day 61** to **Day 80**, use these worksheets to fill in fact families.

13 / 9 + 4

9 + 4 = 13
4 + 9 = 13
13 - 4 = 9
13 - 9 = 4

14 / 9 + 5

9 + 5 = 14
5 + 9 = 14
14 - 5 = 9
14 - 9 = 5

16 / 8 + 8

8 + 8 = 16
___ + ___ = ___
16 - 8 = 8
___ - ___ = ___

17 / 9 + 8

9 + 8 = 17
8 + 9 = 17
17 - 8 = 9
17 - 9 = 8

Day 61+

Fact Families VII

From **Day 61** to **Day 80**, use these worksheets to fill in fact families.

12 / 6 − 6

18 / 9 + 9

6 + 6 = 12

9 + 9 = 18

___ + ___ = ___

___ + ___ = ___

12 − 6 = 6

18 − 9 = 9

___ − ___ = ___

___ − ___ = ___

Day 61

Addition & Subtraction

A. Follow the chain and fill in the ovals.

2 →+3 5 →+4 9 →−3 6 →+7 13

↓+4

6 →+4 10 →−3 7 →+7 14 →−8 6

↓+3

9 →+8 17 →−7 10 →−8 2 →+9 11

↓+5

14 →−6 8 →+5 13 →−9 4 →+8 12

↓−9

5 →+6 11 →−8 3 →+7 10 →−5 5

B. Find the mystery number.

Start with 17, subtract 8, and add 5.   14

Day 62

Addition Word Search

A. Solve the addition problems.

6 + 4 = 10   7 + 6 = 13

7 + 2 = 9   6 + 8 = 14

8 + 7 = 15   9 + 7 = 16

5 + 6 = 11   3 + 5 = 8

9 + 8 = 17   8 + 4 = 12

B. Read the answers as words. Find the words in the puzzle below and circle them. The words go across from left to right and down from top to bottom.

E	G	D	K	F	C	F	B	T	W	E	L	V	E
L	T	E	N	O	X	A	H	H	P	Y	C	Q	J
E	O	J	M	U	Q	Z	F	I	F	T	E	E	N
V	B	C	L	R	B	G	Y	R	K	X	I	Z	I
E	S	I	X	T	E	E	N	T	U	H	G	Q	N
N	N	J	Z	E	X	P	R	E	K	D	H	X	E
G	A	X	P	E	V	F	Q	E	B	U	T	K	A
S	E	V	E	N	T	E	E	N	A	Y	D	M	E

Day 63

Subtraction Matching

Connect the problems to their correct answers.

2   3   4   5   6

8 − 4   7 − 5   11 − 5   6 − 3   10 − 5

3   5   6   4   2

10 − 4   8 − 5   9 − 4   8 − 6   7 − 3

2   5   6   4   8

8 − 3   6 − 4   5 − 2   9 − 3   10 − 6

Day 64

Addition Pyramids

Each number is the sum of the two numbers below it. Fill in the hexagons.

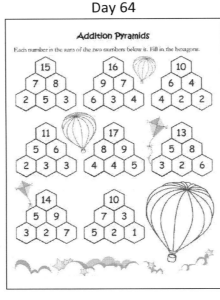

15 / 7 8 / 2 5 3

16 / 9 7 / 6 3 4

10 / 6 4 / 4 2 2

11 / 5 6 / 2 3 3

17 / 8 9 / 4 4 5

13 / 5 8 / 3 2 6

14 / 5 9 / 3 2 7

10 / 7 3 / 5 2 1

Day 65

Tens and Ones

Write the correct number in each blank.

2 tens + 9 ones = 29   5 tens + 0 ones = 50

8 tens + 5 ones = 85   7 tens + 6 ones = 76

4 tens + 3 ones = 43   9 tens + 2 ones = 92

9 tens + 7 ones = 97   3 tens + 4 ones = 34

6 tens + 1 one = 61   1 ten + 8 ones = 18

40	TENS	ONES		38	TENS	ONES
	4	0			3	8
74	TENS	ONES		16	TENS	ONES
	7	4			1	6
92	TENS	ONES		53	TENS	ONES
	9	2			5	3
61	TENS	ONES		29	TENS	ONES
	6	1			2	9

Day 66

Subtraction Puzzles

Solve the subtraction problems. Use your **Fact Families** pages for help.

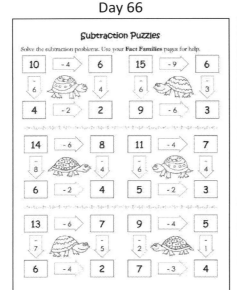

10 −4 6
↓−6
4 −2 2

15 −9 6
↓−4
9 −6 3

14 −6 8
↓−8
6 −2 4

11 −4 7
↓−6
4 −2 3

13 −6 7
↓−8
6 −4 2

9 −4 5
↓−2
7 −3 4

Day 67

Addition Matching

Connect the problems to their correct answers.

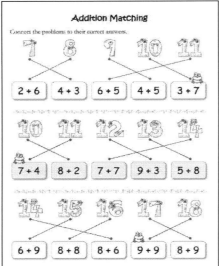

7   8   9   10   11

2 + 6   4 + 3   6 + 5   4 + 5   3 + 7

10   11   12   13   14

7 + 4   8 + 2   7 + 7   9 + 3   5 + 8

14   15   16   17   18

6 + 9   8 + 8   8 + 6   9 + 9   8 + 9

Day 68

Subtraction Maze

Help the dog find its friends. Solve the subtraction problems. Color the sections containing an even answer. You'll find the path!

	7 −3 4	6 −4 2	9 −5 4	6 −3 3
10 −5 5	5 −2 3	8 −3 5	9 −4 5	3 −1 2	8 −5 3
4 −2 2	7 −3 4	9 −1 8	5 −3 2	8 −4 4	9 −4 5
6 −4 2	8 −3 5	10 −5 5	6 −3 3	7 −4 3	10 −9 1
9 −5 4	6 −2 4	4 −2 2	8 −4 4		

Day 69

Addition Crossword

Solve the addition problems and fill in the squares.

2	+	5	=	7
+		+		+
4	+	4	=	8
=		=		=
6	+	9	=	15

3	+	2	=	5
+		+		+
4	+	2	=	6
=		=		=
7	+	4	=	11

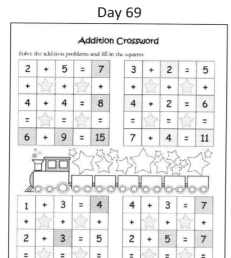

1	+	3	=	4
+		+		+
2	+	3	=	5
=		=		=
3	+	6	=	9

4	+	3	=	7
+		+		+
2	+	5	=	7
=		=		=
6	+	8	=	14

Day 70

Subtraction Maze

Help the turtle find its friends. Solve the subtraction problems and then color the odd answers. You'll find the path!

4 −4 = 0	7 −4 = 3	7 −2 = 5	5 −2 = 3	8 −5 = 3	9 −4 = 5
6 −4 = 2	10 −5 = 5	8 −0 = 8	9 −5 = 4	6 −2 = 4	8 −4 = 4
7 −5 = 2	5 −4 = 1	6 −5 = 1	9 −4 = 5	5 −2 = 3	6 −3 = 3

Day 71

Subtraction Crossword

Fill in the blanks. Use your **Fact Families** pages for help.

16	−	9	=	7
13		9	−	2	=	7
5	−	0	=	5
=				
8	−	2	=	6

14	−	8	=	6
		−
11			2
7	−	3	=	4
15	−	8	=	7

18		11	−	4	=	7
−		
9	−	7	=	2
=		
9		10	−	7	=	3

8		10
4	−	2	=	2
3		6		8

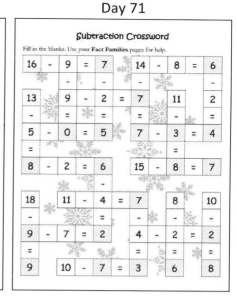

Day 72

Addition Rockets

In each rocket, add the number in the head to each number on the left side. Write the answers on the right side.

+ 9 =

2	11
5	14
8	17
6	15
9	18
3	12
7	16
4	13

+ 8 =

3	11
6	13
9	16
2	10
9	17
8	15
4	12
8	16

+ 7 =

| 7 | 14 |
| 3 | 10 |

+ 6 =

2	8
4	10
7	13
3	9
6	12
9	15
5	11
8	14

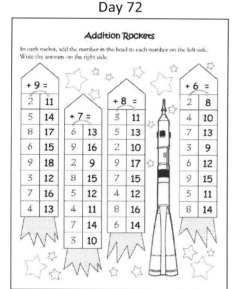

Day 73

Fact Families Review

Review your **Fact Families** pages. Here are some. Fill in the blanks.

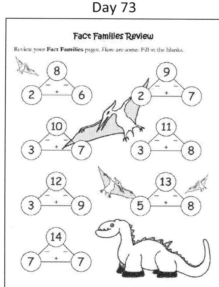

8 − + − 2 + 6

9 + 2 + 7

10 − + 3 + 7

11 − 3 + 8

12 − 3 − 9

13 − 5 + 8

14 − 7 − 7

Day 74

Addition Squares

Add each number in the shaded row to each number in the shaded column. The first one is done for you.

+	4	3
2	6	5
4	8	7

+	6	4
9	15	13
6	12	10

+	8	5
5	13	10
9	17	14

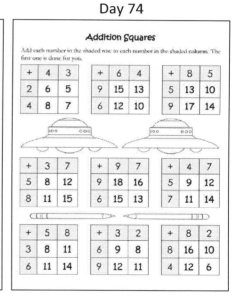

+	3	7
5	8	12
8	11	15

+	9	7
9	18	16
6	15	13

+	4	7
5	9	12
7	11	14

+	5	8
3	8	11
6	11	14

+	3	2
6	9	8
9	12	11

+	8	2
8	16	10
4	12	6

Day 75

Subtraction Maze

Subtract your way through the maze to lead the turtle to its friends.

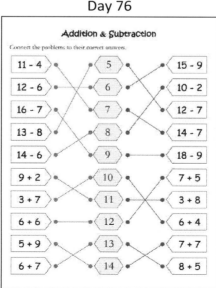

Start 10 − 5 =
8 − 3 =
9 − 4 =
6 − 2 =
7 − 2 =
8 − 4 =
End

Day 76

Addition & Subtraction

Connect the problems to their correct answers.

11 − 4		5		15 − 9
12 − 6		6		10 − 2
16 − 7		7		12 − 7
13 − 8		8		14 − 7
14 − 6		9		18 − 9
9 + 2		10		7 + 5
3 + 7		11		3 + 8
6 + 6		12		6 + 4
5 + 9		13		7 + 7
6 + 7		14		8 + 5

Day 77

Addition & Subtraction

Solve the addition and subtraction problems.

5	+ 6	11	− 2	9	− 3	6
+		−		+		−
12	− 4	8	+ 5	13	− 9	4

7	+ 5	12	− 6	6	+ 4	10
−		−		+		−
4	+ 5	9	+ 2	11	− 8	3

9	+ 6	15	− 9	6	− 3	3
+		−		−		+
14	− 6	8	− 4	4	+ 7	11

Day 79

Shapes & Subtraction

A. Draw lines to match the shapes and their names.

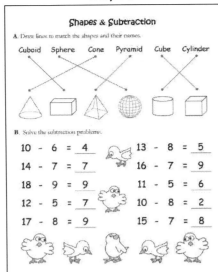

Cuboid   Sphere   Cone   Pyramid   Cube   Cylinder

B. Solve the subtraction problems.

10 - 6 = 4   13 - 8 = 5
14 - 7 = 7   16 - 7 = 9
18 - 9 = 9   11 - 5 = 6
12 - 5 = 7   10 - 8 = 2
17 - 8 = 9   15 - 7 = 8

Day 80

Addition & Subtraction

A. Solve the addition and subtraction problems.

1. 7 + 4 = 11   6. 16 - 8 = 8
2. 9 + 6 = 15   7. 12 - 7 = 5
3. 6 + 7 = 13   8. 10 - 4 = 6
4. 4 + 8 = 12   9. 14 - 5 = 9
5. 7 + 3 = 10   10. 15 - 8 = 7

B. Follow the numbers in the order of your answers above.

		11		17	12	7	3
18	15	4	7				
	13	16		6	9		
10		10	8	5			
	12		9		1		7
15	14	7	6				Finish

Day 81+

Daily Practice for the Week

From Day 81 to Day 85, solve one row of problems each day.

9	8	8	5	9	5	7	2
+5	+6	+7	+6	+9	+8	+3	+9
14	14	15	11	18	13	10	11

14	17	11	12	16	10	13	15
-8	-9	-4	-7	-8	-6	-4	-7
6	8	7	5	8	4	9	8

8	4	3	9	2	7	8	7
+9	+7	+8	+4	+7	+6	+8	+9
17	11	13	9	13	16	16	

15	12	14	9	18	13	10	16
-6	-4	-7	-6	-9	-4	-3	-7
9	8	7	3	9	7	9	

7	3	6	2	7	6	4	
+7	+9	+9	+8	+5	+6	+4	
14	12	15	10	12	12	12	10

Day 81

Word Problems

Solve each word problem. Use the space on the right for your work area.

Mark rode his bike 7 miles to the library. Then he rode 5 miles to the park. How many miles did Mark ride altogether?

12 miles   7 + 5 = 12

Samantha went to the park. She saw 8 birds on one tree and 6 birds on another tree. How many birds did Samantha see altogether?

14 birds   8 + 6 = 14

Mom went to the grocery store. She bought 6 red apples and 5 green apples. How many apples did she buy altogether?

11 apples   6 + 5 = 11

Day 82

Word Problems

Solve each word problem. Use the space on the right for your work area.

William ate 6 grapes. Ethan ate 4 more grapes than William. How many grapes did Ethan eat?

10 grapes   6 + 4 = 10

Daniel found 9 ladybugs in the yard. Emily found 5 more ladybugs than Daniel. How many ladybugs did Emily find?

14 ladybugs   9 + 5 = 14

At the garden, Emma planted 8 flowers. Olivia planted 8 more flowers than Emma. How many flowers did Olivia plant?

16 flowers   8 + 8 = 16

Day 83

Word Problems

Solve each word problem. Use the space on the right for your work area.

Abigail gave 5 candies to her sister Jenny. Now she only has 9 candies. How many candies did Abigail have at first?

14 candies   9 + 5 = 14

Derek gave 4 stickers to his sister Mia. Now he only has 6 stickers. How many stickers did Derek have at first?

10 stickers   6 + 4 = 10

Claire gave 6 pencils to her brother Noah. Now she only has 7 pencils. How many pencils did Claire have at first?

13 pencils   7 + 6 = 13

Day 84

Word Problems

Solve each word problem. Use the space on the right for your work area.

Henry and Anne have 15 books together. 6 of the books belong to Henry. How many books does Anne have?

9 books   15 - 6 = 9

Altogether, Jacob and Orson have 12 toy cars. 8 of the toy cars belong to Jacob. How many toy cars does Orson have?

4 toy cars   12 - 8 = 4

At the apple farm, Owen and Grace picked 16 apples together. Owen picked 9 apples. How many apples did Grace pick?

7 apples   16 - 9 = 7

Day 85

Word Problems

Solve each word problem. Use the space on the right for your work area.

Naomi had 8 toy cars. Her parents gave her 3 more toy cars for her birthday. How many toy cars did Naomi have then?

11 toy cars   8 + 3 = 11

Larry saved $7 last week. He got his allowance on Monday and saved $7 more. How much did Larry have then?

14 dollars   7 + 7 = 14

Angela read 8 pages of her storybook yesterday. She read 8 more pages today. How many pages did Angela read altogether?

16 pages   8 + 8 = 16

Day 86+

Daily Practice for the Week

From Day 86 to Day 90, solve one row of problems each day.

15	13	17	11	14	12	16	8
-9	-8	-9	-5	-4	-5	-9	-6
6	5	8	6	10	7	7	2

4	7	3	8	5	2	6	9
+4	+7	+3	+8	+5	+2	+6	+9
8	14	6	16	10	4	12	18

10	11	13	9	12	11	16	13
-7	-3	-9	-5	-8	-7	-8	-7
3	8	4	4	4	4	8	6

9	8	6	9	7	9	5	6
+8	+5	+5	+7	+8	+6	+7	+7
17	13	11	16	15	15	12	13

10	14	15	12	9	11	10	14
-4	-7	-8	-3	-7	-9	-2	-6
6	7	7	9	2	2	8	8

Day 86

Word Problems
Solve each word problem. Use the space on the right for your work area.

15 children watched the baseball game. 8 children were wearing hats. How many children were not wearing hats?

7 children   15 − 8 = 7

13 flowers are in the garden. 9 flowers are pink and the rest are yellow and white. How many flowers are not pink?

4 flowers   13 − 9 = 4

12 apples are in the basket. 8 apples are red and the rest are green. How many apples are green?

4 apples   12 − 8 = 4

Day 87

Word Problems
Solve each word problem. Use the space on the right for your work area.

Kate had 7 pairs of socks. Her grandmother gave her 5 more pairs. How many pairs of socks did she have then?

12 pairs of socks   7 + 5 = 12

Dylan had 8 blue pencils. His older brother gave him 6 more pencils. How many pencils did Dylan have then?

14 pencils   8 + 6 = 14

Amber had 6 smiley stickers. Her sister gave her 9 more stickers. How many stickers did Amber have then?

15 stickers   6 + 9 = 15

Day 88

Word Problems
Solve each word problem. Use the space on the right for your work area.

11 children were wearing blue hats. 5 children were wearing red hats. How many more children were wearing blue hats?

6 children   11 − 5 = 6

Leah read 18 pages of her story book. Mark read 9 pages of his story book. How many more pages did Leah read?

9 pages   18 − 9 = 9

Sam has 14 red marbles. Mason has 7 blue marbles. How many more marbles does Sam have?

7 marbles   14 − 7 = 7

Day 89

Word Problems
Solve each word problem. Use the space on the right for your work area.

14 ducks were swimming in the pond. 6 ducks flew away. How many ducks were still swimming in the pond?

8 ducks   14 − 6 = 8

11 children were wearing hats. 4 children took their hats off. How many children were still wearing their hats?

7 children   11 − 4 = 7

Alice had 12 candies. She gave 6 candies to her brother. How many candies did Alice still have?

6 candies   12 − 6 = 8

Day 90

Word Problems
Solve each word problem. Use the space on the right for your work area.

At the ball game, 7 children jumped up and cheered for the players. 5 more children joined them. How many children were cheering then?

12 children   7 + 5 = 12

8 children were reading in the library. 9 more children joined them. How many children were reading in the library then?

17 children   8 + 9 = 17

9 ducks were swimming in the pond. 6 ducks flew in and landed in the pond. How many ducks were swimming in the pond then?

15 ducks   9 + 6 = 15

Day 91+

Daily Practice for the Week
From **Day 91** to **Day 95**, solve one row of problems each day.

6 +8	5 +3	8 +9	5 +4	7 +6	4 +9	3 +7	9 +6
14	**8**	**17**	**9**	**13**	**13**	**10**	**15**
13 −6	15 −8	12 −4	14 −9	12 −3	18 −9	13 −4	16 −8
7	**7**	**8**	**5**	**9**	**9**	**9**	**8**
5 +9	8 +4	7 +7	4 +6	9 +9	8 +3	6 +6	8 +7
14	**12**	**14**	**10**	**18**	**11**	**12**	**15**
17 −8	13 −5	14 −7	15 −6	12 −5	13 −4	16 −7	14 −8
9	**8**	**7**	**9**	**7**	**9**	**9**	**6**
6 +5	9 +7	6 +3	8 +5	7 +4	3 +9	8 +8	5 +7
11	**16**	**9**	**13**	**11**	**12**	**16**	**12**

Day 91

Identifying Coins

A. Find all the pennies and color them brown.

B. Match the picture, name, and value of the coins.

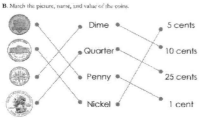

Dime   5 cents
Quarter   10 cents
Penny   25 cents
Nickel   1 cent

C. Match the front, back, and value of the coins.

5 cents
10 cents
1 cent

Day 92

Counting Coins
Use this hundreds chart to help you count coins.

1	2	3	4	5	6	7	8	9	10
11	12	13	14	15	16	17	18	19	20
21	22	23	24	25	26	27	28	29	30
31	32	33	34	35	36	37	38	39	40
41	42	43	44	45	46	47	48	49	50
51	52	53	54	55	56	57	58	59	60
61	62	63	64	65	66	67	68	69	70
71	72	73	74	75	76	77	78	79	80
81	82	83	84	85	86	87	88	89	90
91	92	93	94	95	96	97	98	99	100

A. Count 2 dimes and 3 pennies. How much money do you have?   23 ¢

B. Count 3 dimes and 3 nickels. How much money do you have?   45 ¢

C. Count 1 dime, 3 nickels, and 2 pennies. How much money do you have?   27 ¢

D. Count 2 dimes, 3 nickels, and 4 pennies. How much money do you have?   39 ¢

Day 93

Matching Money

A. Draw lines to match the same amounts.

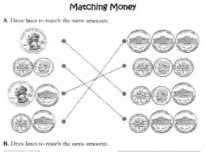

B. Draw lines to match the same amounts.

$ .55		3 nickels + 4 pennies
$ .27		3 dimes + 6 pennies
$ .19		2 quarters + 1 nickel
$ .80		5 dimes + 6 nickels
$ .36		1 quarter + 2 pennies

Day 94

Counting Coins

Color all the pennies brown. Count the coins and write the amounts in cents.

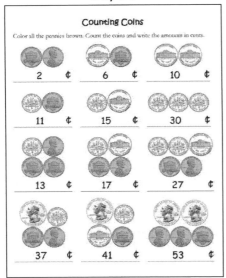

2 ¢ 6 ¢ 10 ¢

11 ¢ 15 ¢ 30 ¢

13 ¢ 17 ¢ 27 ¢

37 ¢ 41 ¢ 53 ¢

Day 96+

Daily Practice for the Week

From **Day 96** to **Day 100**, solve one row of problems each day.

12	14	18	10	9	13	11	16
- 7	- 6	- 9	- 6	- 6	- 9	- 5	- 7
5	8	9	4	3	4	6	9

8	6	9	6	4	7	6	7
+ 8	+ 7	+ 9	+ 5	+ 9	+ 7	+ 9	+ 8
16	13	18	11	13	14	15	15

11	15	13	8	14	10	12	17
- 4	- 7	- 5	- 2	- 7	- 3	- 8	- 9
7	8	8	6	7	7	4	8

7	5	6	9	7	8	6	9
+ 9	+ 7	+ 8	+ 5	+ 4	+ 5	+ 6	+ 8
16	12	14	14	11	13	12	17

16	12	9	13	11	15	10	14
- 8	- 6	- 7	- 4	- 8	- 9	- 2	- 5
8	6	2	9	3	6	8	9

Day 96

Picking a Coin

Color all the pennies brown. Which coin do you need to make 25 cents?

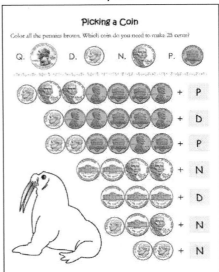

Q.   D.   N.   P.

+ P
+ D
+ P
+ N
+ D
+ N
+ N

Day 97

Counting Coins

Color all the pennies brown. Count the coins and write the amounts in cents.

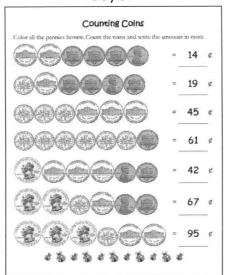

= 14 ¢
= 19 ¢
= 45 ¢
= 61 ¢
= 42 ¢
= 67 ¢
= 95 ¢

Day 98

Buying Items

Find all the pennies and color them brown. Do you have the **exact** amount of money needed to buy each item? Circle **YES** or **NO**.

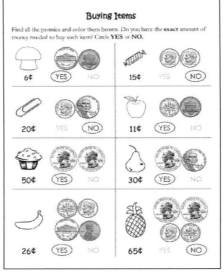

6¢ — YES / NO   15¢ — YES / NO

20¢ — YES / NO   11¢ — YES / NO

50¢ — YES / NO   30¢ — YES / NO

26¢ — YES / NO   65¢ — YES / NO

Day 99

Buying Items

Use the fewest number of coins to buy each item for the exact amount.

Items				
7¢	0	0	1	2
14¢	0	1	0	4
22¢	0	2	0	2
28¢	1	0	0	3
30¢	1	0	1	0
60¢	2	1	0	0

Day 100

Buying Items

Use the fewest number of coins to buy each item for the exact amount.

Items				
29¢	1	0	0	4
33¢	1	0	1	3
42¢	1	1	1	2
58¢	2	0	1	3
67¢	2	1	1	2
96¢	3	2	0	1

Day 101+

Daily Practice for the Week

From **Day 101** to **Day 105**, solve one row of problems each day.

4	7	6	7	3	5	7	8
+ 9	+ 7	+ 4	+ 9	+ 5	+ 6	+ 3	+ 8
13	14	10	16	8	11	10	16

14	18	11	13	16	10	12	15
- 7	- 9	- 6	- 5	- 7	- 4	- 9	- 6
7	9	5	8	9	6	3	9

7	5	9	8	8	7	8	6
+ 8	+ 4	+ 9	+ 3	+ 5	+ 6	+ 4	+ 9
15	9	18	11	13	13	12	15

13	16	15	10	12	14	11	17
- 4	- 8	- 7	- 8	- 7	- 5	- 3	- 8
9	8	8	2	5	9	8	9

9	4	6	8	3	5	8	6
+ 5	+ 7	+ 3	+ 6	+ 9	+ 7	+ 9	+ 6
14	11	9	14	12	12	17	12

Day 101

Word Problems

Solve each word problem. Use the space on the right for your work area.

Liam has $6. Stella has $8 more than Liam. How much money does Stella have?

14 dollars   6 + 8 = 14

Kim has 7 pencils. Max has 3 more pencils than Kim. How many pencils does Max have?

10 pencils   7 + 3 = 10

Sam rode his bike 9 miles. Ron rode 4 more miles than Sam. How many miles did Ron ride?

13 miles   9 + 4 = 13

Day 102

Word Problems

Solve each word problem. Use the space on the right for your work area.

Ava learned 6 new spelling words this week. She learned 9 new words last week. How many new words did Ava learn altogether?

15 new words $6 + 9 = 15$

Adam read 8 pages of his book today. He read 5 pages yesterday. How many pages did Adam read altogether?

13 pages $8 + 5 = 13$

Kyle jumped a rope 9 times on the first try. He jumped 8 times on the second try. How many times did Kyle jump altogether?

17 times $9 + 8 = 17$

Day 103

Word Problems

Solve each word problem. Use the space on the right for your work area.

At a grocery store, a bag of apples costs $4 less than a bag of oranges. A bag of oranges costs $11. How much does a bag of apples cost?

7 dollars $11 - 4 = 7$

Thomas saw 13 butterflies in the yard. Ella saw 5 fewer butterflies than Thomas. How many butterflies did Ella see?

8 butterflies $13 - 5 = 8$

At the orchard, Richard picked 16 apples. Cooper picked 9 fewer apples than Richard. How many apples did Cooper pick?

7 apples $16 - 9 = 7$

Day 104

Word Problems

Solve each word problem. Use the space on the right for your work area.

Gary has 12 stickers. Will has 9 stickers. How many more stickers does Gary have than Will?

3 stickers $12 - 9 = 3$

Julia has $10. Hunter has $6. How much more does Julia have than Hunter?

4 dollars $10 - 6 = 4$

Jack has 11 marbles. Eva has 5 marbles. How many more marbles does Jack have than Eva?

6 marbles $11 - 5 = 6$

Day 105

Word Problems

Solve each word problem. Use the space on the right for your work area.

Amber is 9 years old. Amber's sister Allison is 6 years older. How old is Allison?

15 years old $9 + 6 = 15$

Maya is 5 years old. Maya's brother Joe is 4 years older. How old is Joe?

9 years old $5 + 4 = 9$

Michael is 7 years old. Michael's sister Claire is 7 years older. How old is Claire?

14 years old $7 + 7 = 14$

Day 106+

Daily Practice for the Week

From **Day 106** to **Day 116**, solve one row of problems each day.

12	18	14	10	9	11	13	16
- 4	- 9	- 5	- 2	- 6	- 5	- 6	- 9
8	9	9	8	3	6	7	7

4	7	5	7	6	9	5	8
+ 9	+ 7	+ 8	+ 2	+ 7	+ 9	+ 4	+ 7
13	14	13	9	13	18	9	15

14	12	15	10	11	17	9	13
- 7	- 6	- 9	- 6	- 4	- 9	- 2	- 8
7	6	6	4	7	8	7	5

3	5	8	6	8	7	5	9
+ 6	+ 9	+ 2	+ 5	+ 8	+ 5	+ 5	+ 7
9	14	10	11	16	12	10	16

15	11	13	14	11	10	16	12
- 8	- 2	- 9	- 8	- 8	- 3	- 8	- 5
7	9	4	6	3	7	8	7

Day 106

Making a Dollar

A. One dollar is worth 100 cents. There are many ways to make one dollar using coins. Color all the piggy banks that contain exactly one dollar.

100 pennies   6 dimes + 40 pennies

10 dimes   2 quarters + 3 dimes

8 dimes   3 quarters + 5 nickels

4 quarters   4 dimes + 8 nickels

20 nickels   2 quarters + 5 dimes

B. Count the bills and coins. Write the total amount of money.

 = $ 1.22

= $ 5.26

 = $ 10.35

Day 107

Counting Coins

Color all the pennies brown. Count the coins and write the amounts in cents.

= 18 ¢

= 22 ¢

= 65 ¢

= 52 ¢

= 30 ¢

= 80 ¢

= 86 ¢

Day 108

Comparing Money

Color all the pennies brown. Compare the amounts with >, <, or =.

 <

 =

 >

 <

=

Day 109

Counting Money

Color all the pennies brown. Write the total amount of money.

= $ 5.25

= $ 10.35

= $ 11.45

= $ 10.21

= $ 15.40

= $ 26.30

Day 110

Counting Money

Color all the pennies brown. Write the total amount of money.

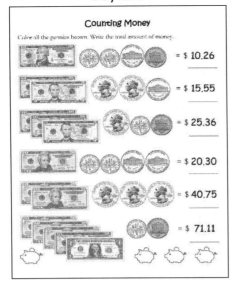

= $ 10.26

= $ 15.55

= $ 25.36

= $ 20.30

= $ 40.75

= $ 71.11

Day 111

Money Word Problems

Read each story problem. Write the answer.

Mark has 1 dime. Samantha has 8 pennies. How much money do they have altogether? — 18 ¢

William has 2 nickels. Ethan has 2 pennies. How much money do they have altogether? — 12 ¢

Daniel has 4 dimes. He finds 2 more dimes. How much money does Daniel have in all? — 60 ¢

Emily has 2 quarters. She finds 1 more quarter. How much money does Emily have in all? — 75 ¢

Emma bought an apple for 1 quarter and a key for 2 nickels. How much money did Emma spend in all? — 35 ¢

Olivia had 10¢ until she spent 4 pennies on a whistle. How much money does Olivia have now? — 6 ¢

Abigail had 14¢ until she spent 1 nickel on a yo-yo. How much money does Abigail have now? — 9 ¢

Jenny had 50¢ until she spent 2 dimes on a hat. How much money does Jenny have now? — 30 ¢

Day 112

Money Word Problems

Read each story problem. Write the answer.

Henry has 4 pennies in one hand and 3 dimes in the other hand. How much money does he have in all? — 34 ¢

Claire has 2 nickels. She finds 3 more nickels. How much money does she have in all? — 25 ¢

Derek has 1 nickel. Mia has 7 pennies. How much money do they have altogether? — 12 ¢

Anne has 3 dimes. Paul has 5 pennies. Who has more money? — Anne

Jacob bought a pear for 2 quarters and a candy for 8 pennies. How much money did Jacob spend in all? — 58 ¢

Orson had 20¢ until he spent 5 pennies on a LEGO block. How much money does Orson have now? — 15 ¢

Owen had 42¢ until he spent 2 dimes on an ice cream cone. How much money does Owen have now? — 22 ¢

Grace had 50¢ until she spent 1 quarter on glue. How much money does Grace have now? — 25 ¢

Day 113

Money Word Problems

Read each story problem. Write the answer.

What is the total of 25¢ and 40¢? — 65 ¢

What is 30¢ less than 64¢? — 34 ¢

Angela collects nickels and has 35¢ worth. How many nickels does Angela have? — 7

Larry has 2 quarters and 4 dimes. How much does he need to make a dollar? — 10 ¢

Mary had 65¢ but lost 20¢. How much does she have left? — 45 ¢

Paul has 4 coins that add up to 17¢. Which coins does Paul have? — 10 ¢ 5 ¢ 1 ¢ 1 ¢

80¢ is shared equally by four children. How much money does each child get? — 20 ¢

How much money is four groups of coins with 1 dime and 2 nickels in each group? — 80 ¢

5 nickels and 3 pennies are shared equally by two children. How much money does each child get? — 14 ¢

Day 114

Money Word Problems

Read the story and answer the questions below.

Kate, Dylan, and Amber went to a toy store. Kate had 2 quarters and 1 dime. Dylan had 5 nickels and 5 pennies. Amber had 4 dimes and 6 pennies. At the toy store, they saw these items:

Whistle	Candy	Toy Car	Dice	Top
20¢	15¢	50¢	4¢	35¢

1. How much money does each one have?

Kate — 60 ¢   Dylan — 30 ¢   Amber — 46 ¢

1. Kate bought one whistle and two candies. How much money did Kate spend in all? — 50 ¢

2. Dylan wants to buy a toy car. How much more money will he need? — 20 ¢

3. Amber bought a top. How much money does she have left? — 11 ¢

4. How much money did Kate and Amber spend altogether? — 85 ¢

Day 115

Addition & Subtraction

Solve the addition and subtraction problems.

3	+	7	=	10		15	-	9	=	6
		-						-		+
18		2	+	6	=	8		13		6
-		=				=		-		=
9	-	5	=	4		7	+	5	=	12
=										=
9	+	3	=	12		8	+	8	=	16
14		15	-	8	=	7		13		8
-				+				+		+
8	-	4	=	4		7	-	4	=	3
=				=				=		=
6		5	+	9	=	14		9		11

Day 116+

Daily Practice for the Week

From Day 116 to Day 120, solve one row of problems each day.

14	11	16	13	15	10	17	12
- 5	- 8	- 7	- 8	- 7	- 6	- 8	- 6
9	3	9	5	8	4	9	6

4	9	8	5	9	4	5	7
+ 8	+ 6	+ 8	+ 7	+ 9	+ 6	+ 4	+ 9
12	15	16	12	18	10	9	16

11	13	10	18	9	14	15	12
- 4	- 9	- 3	- 9	- 6	- 9	- 6	- 7
7	4	7	9	3	7	9	5

7	9	5	4	8	4	6	9
+ 7	+ 5	+ 5	+ 7	+ 6	+ 7	+ 6	+ 8
14	14	10	11	14	15	12	17

13	10	12	14	10	15	13	11
- 6	- 2	- 4	- 8	- 7	- 8	- 5	- 5
7	8	8	6	3	7	8	6

Day 116

Telling Time: To the Half Hour

What time is it? Circle the correct time.

(3:00) 5:00

(7:00) 11:00

6:00 (10:00)

(3:30) 6:30

(7:30) 9:30

6:30 (10:30)

Color Me!

1:30 (4:30)

(2:30) 4:30

Day 117

Telling Time: 5 Minute Intervals

A. Count by 5s around the clock. Fill in the blanks to show the number of minutes in one hour.

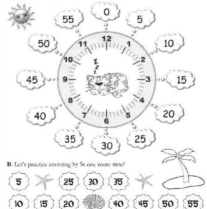

55 0 5
50 10
45 15
40 20
35 30 25

B. Let's practice counting by 5s one more time!

5 — 25 30 35
10 15 20 40 45 50 55

Day 118

Telling Time: To the Quarter Hour
What time is it? Circle the correct time.

(1:15) 1:45   7:30 (7:45)   3:15 (3:45)

6:00 (12:30)   3:45 (9:15)   (2:45) 9:15

6:15 (6:45)   Color Me!   (11:15) 11:45

Day 119

Telling Time: To the Quarter Hour
Draw lines to match each clock with the correct time.

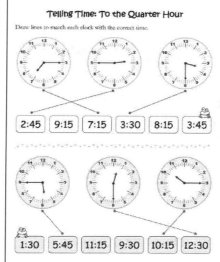

2:45   9:15   7:15   3:30   8:15   3:45

1:30   5:45   11:15   9:30   10:15   12:30

Day 120

Telling Time: To the 5 Minutes
What time is it? Circle the correct time.

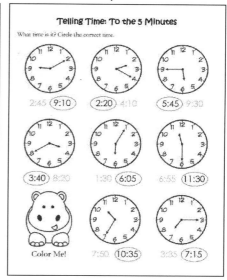

2:45 (9:10)   (2:20) 4:10   (5:45) 9:30

(3:40) 8:20   1:30 (6:05)   6:55 (11:30)

Color Me!   7:50 (10:35)   3:35 (7:15)

Day 121+

Daily Practice for the Week
From Day 121 to Day 125, solve one row of problems each day.

6 +9	8 +7	4 +8	9 +9	6 +8	9 +5	9 +3	7 +9
15	15	12	18	14	14	12	16

17 -8	15 -6	12 -4	14 -5	10 -7	11 -3	16 -9	13 -6
9	9	8	9	3	8	7	7

4 +9	8 +5	9 +8	8 +4	5 +9	8 +8	3 +9	9 +6
13	13	17	12	14	16	12	15

16 -8	10 -4	14 -6	12 -6	18 -9	13 -5	11 -5	15 -7
8	6	8	6	9	8	6	8

7 +8	9 +7	3 +8	8 +6	7 +7	9 +4	5 +8	8 +9
15	16	11	14	14	13	13	17

Day 121

Telling Time: To the 5 Minutes
Draw the hands on each clock face to show the time.

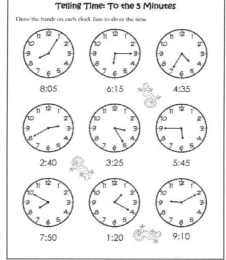

8:05   6:15   4:35

2:40   3:25   5:45

7:50   1:20   9:10

Day 122

Time Passages: To the Hour
Write the time under the clock on the left. Read the word problem and write the new time and then draw the time on the blank clock.

In 2 hours the time will be

11:20   1:20

3 hours ago the time was

8:30   5:30

In 6 hours the time will be

5:15   11:15

Day 123

Time Word Problems
Solve each word problem. The first one is done for you!

It's 9:00 a.m. now. What time will be in 2 hours?   11:00 (a.m.) p.m.

It's 1:00 p.m. now. Leah has soccer practice in 3 hours. What time will practice start?   4:00 a.m. (p.m.)

Leah will practice soccer for 2 hours. What time will practice end?   6:00 a.m. (p.m.)

It's 2:00 p.m. now. Leah will eat dinner 5 hours later. What time will Leah eat dinner?   7:00 a.m. (p.m.)

Leah's favorite TV show ends at 9:00 p.m. She watches it for 1 hour. When does it start?   8:00 a.m. (p.m.)

Leah goes to bed at 9:30 p.m. and gets up at 7:30 a.m. How many hours does she sleep?   10 hours

Leah gets up at 7:30 a.m. Her art class starts in 2 hours. When does her art class start?   9:30 (a.m.) p.m.

Leah eats lunch 3 hours after her art class starts. What time does Leah eat lunch?   12:30 a.m. (p.m.)

Leah reads a book from 10:30 a.m. to 12:30 p.m. How many hours does she read?   2 hours

Day 124

Telling Time: 5 Minutes Later
Sit down with someone who can tell time. Read the time on each clock. Say what time it is going to be in five minutes.

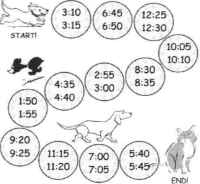

START!

3:10 / 3:15   6:45 / 6:50   12:25 / 12:30

10:05 / 10:10

2:55 / 3:00   8:30 / 8:35

4:35 / 4:40

1:50 / 1:55

9:20 / 9:25   11:15 / 11:20   7:00 / 7:05   5:40 / 5:45   END!

To play it as a game: Take turns. The player rolls the dice and moves forward to land on a clock. The player reads the time and tells what the time will be in five minutes. If the player is incorrect, move back two places. Play continues until all players have reached the end.

Day 125

Time Passages: To the Half Hour
Draw the clock hands to show the passage of time.

What time will it be in 4 hours 0 minutes?   What time will it be in 8 hours 0 minutes?

What time will it be in 2 hours 30 minutes?   What time will it be in 3 hours 30 minutes?

What time will it be in 3 hours 30 minutes?   What time will it be in 5 hours 0 minutes?

Day 126+

Daily Practice for the Week

From Day 126 to Day 130, solve one row of problems each day.

4 +4 = **8**	6 +6 = **12**	2 +2 = **4**	9 +9 = **18**	7 +7 = **14**	3 +3 = **6**	8 +8 = **16**	5 +5 = **10**
15 -6 = **9**	12 -6 = **6**	17 -8 = **9**	10 -3 = **7**	14 -7 = **7**	11 -4 = **7**	13 -5 = **8**	16 -9 = **7**
7 +8 = **15**	8 +4 = **12**	5 +7 = **12**	9 +8 = **17**	3 +9 = **13**	9 +4 = **13**	8 +5 = **13**	6 +9 = **15**
16 -8 = **8**	14 -5 = **9**	11 -3 = **8**	13 -8 = **5**	10 -4 = **6**	18 -9 = **9**	12 -4 = **8**	15 -7 = **8**
3 +8 = **11**	7 +9 = **16**	6 +5 = **11**	3 +9 = **12**	6 +8 = **14**	4 +7 = **11**	9 +5 = **14**	7 +6 = **13**

Day 126

Word Problems

Solve each word problem. Use the space on the right for your work area.

It's 8:00 o'clock in the morning. Lunch is served at 12 o'clock. How many hours until lunch time?
4 hours   12 − 8 = 4

15 kids were in the room. 7 kids left. How many kids were in the room then?
8 kids   15 − 7 = 8

Mark spent $5 on a yo-yo and $8 on a book. How much did Mark spend?
13 dollars   5 + 8 = 13

Sam has 18 dimes. Mason has 9 dimes. How many more dimes does Sam have than Mason?
9 dimes   18 − 9 = 9

Alice saved $6 last week and $7 this week. How much did Alice save in all?
13 dollars   6 + 7 = 13

Day 127

Counting Money

A. Color all the pennies brown. Write the total amount of money.

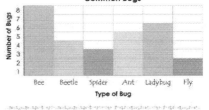

= $ 40.75

= $ 25.40

= $ 7.27

B. Use the fewest number of coins to buy each item for the exact amount.

Items	25¢	10¢	5¢	1¢
8¢	0	0	1	3
17¢	0	1	1	2
42¢	1	1	1	2

Day 128

Reading Graphs

A. Use the bar graph below to answer the questions.

Pets on My Street
Number of Families / Type of Pet

1. How many families have a cat? **3** families
2. How many families have a fish? **2** families
3. How many more families have a bird than a turtle? **3** families
4. How many families have a pet of some type? **13** families

B. Use the pictograph below to answer the questions.

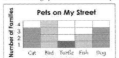

Name	Number of Books Read
Max	📖📖📖📖
Ron	📖📖📖
Ava	📖📖📖📖📖
Sam	📖

KEY 📖 = 2 Books

1. How many books did Sam read? **6** books
2. How many books did Max read? **8** books
3. How many books did Ava read? **10** books
4. How many more books did Ava read than Ron? **6** books
5. How many books did Max and Sam read in all? **14** books
6. How many books did they read altogether? **28** books

Day 129

Pets Bar Graph

Liam asked his friends what kinds of pets they own. The tally chart shows their answers. Make a bar graph to represent the data from the tally chart.

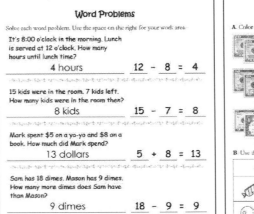

Popular Pets
Number of Pets / Type of Pet

1. How many animals are there in all? **25**
2. How many cats and dogs are there in all? **12**
3. How many birds and fish are there in all? **10**
4. How many more cats are there than turtles? **4**

Day 130

Bugs Bar Graph

The tally chart shows the number of bugs Stella found in her backyard. Make a bar graph to represent the data from the tally chart.

Common Bugs
Number of Bugs / Type of Bug
Bee · Beetle · Spider · Ant · Ladybug · Fly

1. How many bugs are there in all? **28**
2. How many bees and beetles are there in all? **12**
3. How many ants and ladybugs are there in all? **11**
4. How many more bees are there than spiders? **5**

Day 131+

Daily Practice for the Week

From Day 131 to Day 135, solve one row of problems each day.

12 -6 = **6**	15 -8 = **7**	10 -6 = **4**	13 -7 = **6**	11 -5 = **6**	9 -2 = **7**	18 -9 = **9**	14 -7 = **7**
7 +6 = **13**	4 +9 = **13**	5 +4 = **9**	6 +5 = **11**	8 +7 = **15**	3 +9 = **12**	5 +7 = **12**	9 +8 = **17**
16 -7 = **9**	11 -4 = **7**	14 -6 = **8**	9 -0 = **9**	17 -8 = **9**	12 -4 = **8**	10 -3 = **7**	13 -8 = **5**
8 +5 = **13**	6 +9 = **15**	8 +8 = **16**	2 +5 = **7**	6 +6 = **12**	7 +4 = **11**	9 +2 = **11**	6 +8 = **14**
15 -6 = **9**	13 -4 = **9**	10 -7 = **3**	14 -5 = **9**	12 -9 = **3**	11 -3 = **8**	16 -8 = **8**	12 -5 = **7**

Day 131

Favorite Pets Bar Graph

Kim asked her friends to vote for their favorite pets. The tally chart shows their answers. Make a bar graph to represent the data from the tally chart.

Dog	Cat	Hamster	Fish	Snake
卌卌	卌 I	III	I	IIII

Favorite Pets
Number of Votes / Type of Pet
Dog · Cat · Hamster · Fish · Snake

1. Which pet received the most number of votes? **Dog**
2. Which pet received the least number of votes? **Fish**
4. How many friends voted for snake? **4**
5. How many friends voted altogether? **22**
6. How many more votes did dog receive than fish? **7**

Day 132

Books Pictograph

The pictograph below shows the number of books Max and his friends read last month. Use the graph to answer the questions.

Name	Number of Books
Max	📖📖📖📖📖📖
Sam	📖📖📖
Ron	📖📖📖
Ava	📖📖📖📖

KEY 📖 = 2 Books

1. Who read the most number of books? **Max**
2. Who read the least number of books? **Ron**
3. How many books did Sam read? **7**
4. How many books did Ava and Ron read? **13**
5. How many more books did Max read than Ron? **6**
6. How many more books did Sam read than Ava? **0**
7. How many more books did Max read than Ava? **5**
8. How many books did they read altogether? **32**

Day 133

Apples Pictograph

The pictograph below shows the number of apples sold at the local grocery store over 4 months. Use the graph to answer the questions.

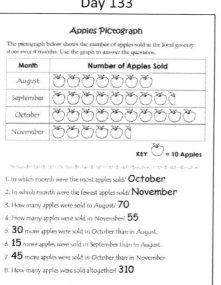

KEY 🍎 = 10 Apples

1. In which month were the most apples sold? **October**
2. In which month were the fewest apples sold? **November**
3. How many apples were sold in August? **70**
4. How many apples were sold in November? **55**
5. **30** more apples were sold in October than in August.
6. **15** more apples were sold in September than in August.
7. **45** more apples were sold in October than in November.
8. How many apples were sold altogether? **310**

Day 134

Desserts Pie Chart

Adam asked his friends to vote for their favorite dessert. The tally chart shows their answers. Make a circle graph to represent the data from the tally chart.

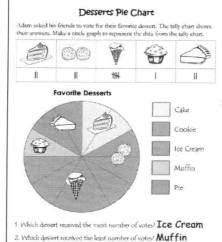

Favorite Desserts

- Cake
- Cookie
- Ice Cream
- Muffin
- Pie

1. Which dessert received the most number of votes? **Ice Cream**
2. Which dessert received the least number of votes? **Muffin**
3. How many friends voted altogether? **12**

Day 136+

Daily Practice for the Week

From Day 136 to Day 140, solve one row of problems each day.

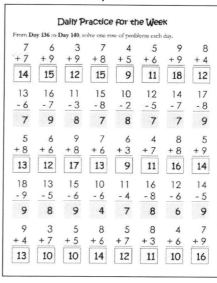

Day 136

Fractions: Halves

A. Color one half of each shape.

B. Circle one half of each group of the animals.

The total number of turtles is __4__   One half is __2__

The total number of ladybugs is __6__   One half is __3__

C. Design your own flags. Color one half of each flag.

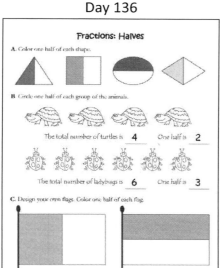

Day 137

Fractions: Fourths

A. Color one fourth of each shape.

B. Circle the fraction that represents the shaded area.

C. Design your own flags. Color three fourths of each flag.

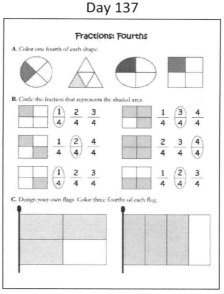

Day 138

Fractions: Thirds

A. Color one third of each shape.

B. Draw lines to complete the sentences.

Thirds means • • 6 equal parts of a whole.
Fourths means • • 8 equal parts of a whole.
Fifths means • • 10 equal parts of a whole.
Sixths means • • 3 equal parts of a whole.
Eighths means • • 5 equal parts of a whole.
Tenths means • • 4 equal parts of a whole.

C. Design your own flags. Color two thirds of each flag.

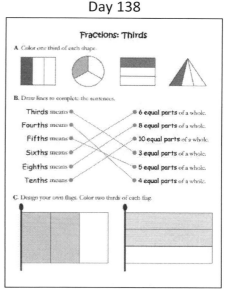

Day 139

Fractions of a Whole

A. Circle the fraction that represents the shaded area.

B. Color in the shape to show the fraction.

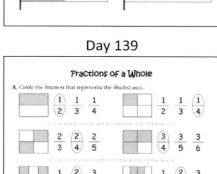

Day 140

Fractions of a Whole

A. Circle the fraction that represents the shaded area.

B. Color in the shape to show the fraction.

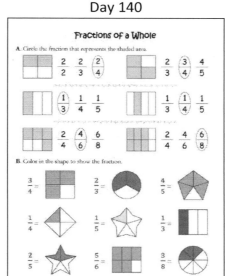

Day 141+

Daily Practice for the Week

From Day 141 to Day 146, solve one row of problems each day.

Day 141

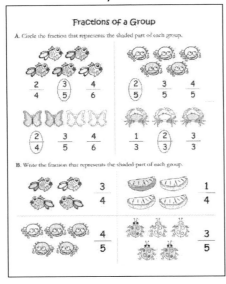

Fractions of a Group

A. Circle the fraction that represents the shaded part of each group.

B. Write the fraction that represents the shaded part of each group.

Day 142

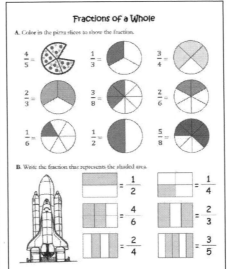

Fractions of a Whole

A. Color in the pizza slices to show the fraction.

B. Write the fraction that represents the shaded area.

Day 143

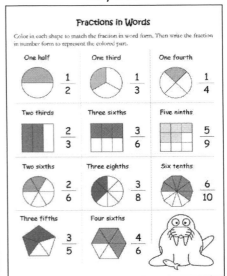

Fractions in Words

Color in each shape to match the fraction in word form. Then write the fraction in number form to represent the colored part.

Day 144

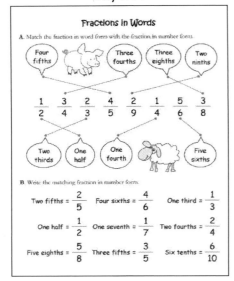

Fractions in Words

A. Match the fraction in word form with the fraction in number form.

B. Write the matching fraction in number form.

Day 145

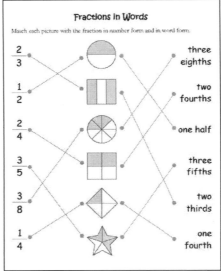

Fractions in Words

Match each picture with the fraction in number form and in word form.

Day 146+

Daily Practice for the Week

From **Day 146** to **Day 150**, solve one row of problems each day.

5	9	4	3	8	6	9	6
+8	+6	+7	+9	+7	+3	+9	+5
13	**15**	**11**	**12**	**15**	**9**	**18**	**11**

15	13	10	18	11	12	16	14
-7	-6	-8	-9	-4	-8	-7	-8
8	**7**	**2**	**9**	**7**	**4**	**9**	**6**

8	5	9	6	4	3	7	5
+8	+5	+8	+6	+8	+7	+6	+9
16	**10**	**17**	**12**	**12**	**10**	**13**	**14**

14	17	12	10	15	13	11	16
-7	-8	-5	-3	-6	-5	-3	-8
7	**9**	**7**	**7**	**9**	**8**	**8**	**8**

9	3	7	4	6	5	4	7
+4	+8	+7	+5	+8	+7	+6	+9
13	**11**	**14**	**9**	**14**	**12**	**10**	**16**

Day 146

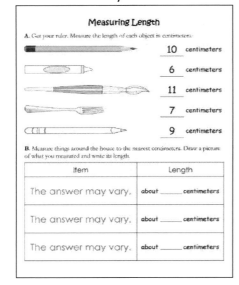

Measuring Length

A. Get your ruler. Measure the length of each object in centimeters.

B. Measure things around the house to the nearest centimeter. Draw a picture of what you measured and write its length.

Day 147

Measuring Length

A. Get your ruler. Measure the length of each object in inches.

B. Measure things around the house to the nearest inches. Draw a picture of what you measured and write its length.

Day 148

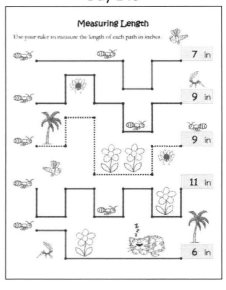

Measuring Length

Use your ruler to measure the length of each path in inches.

Day 149

Reading Temperature

Write the temperature shown on each thermometer.

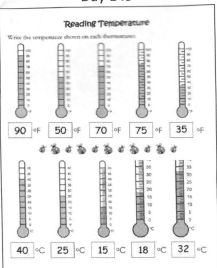

90 °F	50 °F	70 °F	75 °F	35 °F

40 °C	25 °C	15 °C	18 °C	32 °C

Day 150

Guessing Temperature

A. Draw lines to complete the sentences.

The human body is ●　　　　　● 32 °F
Water boils at ●　　　　　● 98 °F
Water freezes at ●　　　　　● 212 °F

B. Read each story. Estimate the temperature and circle your answer.

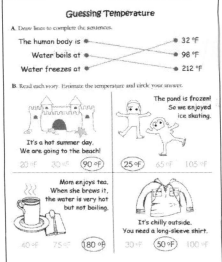

It's a hot summer day. We are going to the beach!
20 °F　　30 °F　　(90 °F)

The pond is frozen! So we enjoyed ice skating.
(25 °F)　　65 °F　　105 °F

Mom enjoys tea. When she brews it, the water is very hot but not boiling.
40 °F　　75 °F　　(180 °F)

It's chilly outside. You need a long-sleeve shirt.
30 °F　　(50 °F)　　100 °F

Day 151+

Daily Practice for the Week

From Day 151 to Day 155, solve one row of problems each day.

17	13	11	15	12	10	14	16
-9	-4	-3	-9	-5	-7	-5	-8
8	9	8	6	7	3	9	8

8	2	5	6	4	5	9	4
+7	+9	+7	+3	+8	+6	+5	+7
15	11	12	9	12	11	14	11

9	12	18	10	14	11	15	13
-2	-8	-9	-4	-9	-4	-8	-5
7	4	9	6	5	7	7	8

7	9	3	7	5	7	8	9
+6	+6	+8	+2	+8	+9	+6	+8
13	15	11	9	13	16	14	17

15	14	9	12	14	12	13	17
-6	-7	-3	-3	-9	-6	-5	-8
9	7	6	9	5	6	8	9

Day 151

Lemonade Bar Graph

Kyle had a lemonade stand. The tally chart shows how many cups of lemonade he sold each day. Make a bar graph to represent the data from the tally chart.

Monday	Tuesday	Wednesday	Thursday	Friday
卌 Ⅲ	Ⅲ	Ⅱ	卌	卌

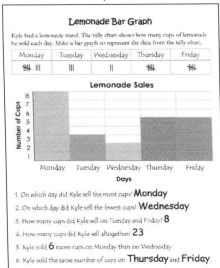

Lemonade Sales

1. On which day did Kyle sell the most cups? **Monday**
2. On which day did Kyle sell the fewest cups? **Wednesday**
3. How many cups did Kyle sell on Tuesday and Friday? **8**
4. How many cups did Kyle sell altogether? **23**
5. Kyle sold **6** more cups on Monday than on Wednesday.
6. Kyle sold the same number of cups on **Thursday** and **Friday**.

Day 152

Counting Coins

Color all the pennies brown. Count the coins and write the amount in cents.

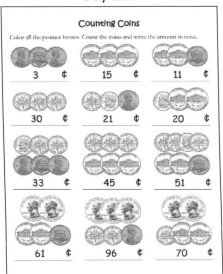

3 ¢	15 ¢	11 ¢
30 ¢	21 ¢	20 ¢
33 ¢	45 ¢	51 ¢
61 ¢	96 ¢	70 ¢

Day 153

Time & Measurements

A. Use your ruler to measure the length of the path in inches.

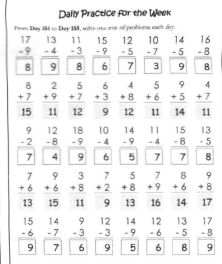

15 in

B. Write the time underneath the clock.

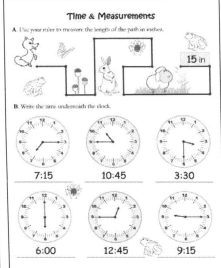

7:15	10:45	3:30
6:00	12:45	9:15

Day 154

Guessing Weight

A. Draw lines to complete the sentences.

A new baby weighs around ●　　　　　● 7 pounds
A cup of milk weighs around ●　　　　　● 1 ounce
A slice of bread weighs around ●　　　　　● 8 ounces

B. Estimate the weight of each object and circle your answer.

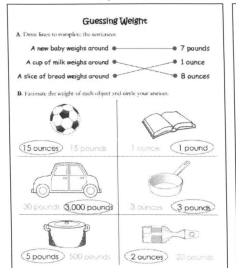

(15 ounces)　15 pounds
1 ounce　(1 pound)
30 pounds　(3,000 pounds)
3 ounces　(3 pounds)
(5 pounds)　500 pounds
(2 ounces)　20 pounds

Day 155

Let's Review!

A. Solve the subtraction problems.

15 - 8 = **7**　　　60 - 20 = **40**
17 - 9 = **8**　　　90 - 30 = **60**

B. Fill in the missing number. Use your 100s chart (Day 92) if you need help.

16	17		38	39		72	73	74
26	27	28	47	48	49	81	82	83	84
	37	38	57	58			92	93

C. Read each question and fill in the blank.

✓ Is 57 closer to 50 or 60? **60**
✓ November is the 11th month. **March** is the **3rd** month.
✓ Ella has **thirteen** stickers. Thomas has **five** stickers. Ella has **8** more stickers than Thomas.

D. Write the number that is ten less than:

7 is ten less than 17
20 is ten less than 30
77 is ten less than 87

E. Write the sum or difference.

6 + 8 = **14**
9 + 4 = **13**
13 - 7 = **6**

Day 156

Let's Review!

A. Read each problem. Which and how many coins does each person have?

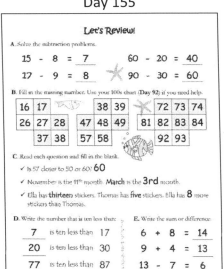

	25¢	10¢	5¢	1¢
Richard has three coins. The total amount is 12¢.	0	1	0	2
Cooper has four coins. The total amount is 25¢.	0	1	3	0
Gary has five coins. The total amount is 37¢.	1	0	2	2

B. Draw the next set of hearts to complete the pattern.

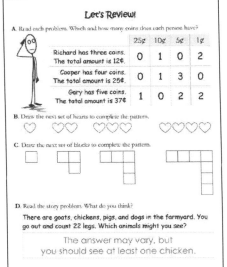

C. Draw the next set of blocks to complete the pattern.

D. Read the story problem. What do you think?

There are goats, chickens, pigs, and dogs in the farmyard. You go out and count 22 legs. Which animals might you see?

The answer may vary, but you should see at least one chicken.

Day 157

Tens and Ones

Count the number of blocks in each set. Write the numbers.

17 25 33

19 22 34

46 58

Day 158

Tens and Ones

Circle the groups of ten. Count the tens and ones. Write the numbers.

1 tens + 8 ones = 18   1 tens + 6 ones = 16

2 tens + 4 ones = 24   2 tens + 0 ones = 20

4 tens + 5 ones = 45   7 tens + 7 ones = 77

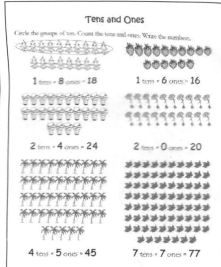

Day 159

Tens and Ones

A. Write the correct number of tens and ones for each number.

	TENS	ONES			TENS	ONES
64	6	4		90	9	0
73	7	3		28	2	8
96	9	6		31	3	1
12	1	2		45	4	5

B. What is the value of the gray digit? Circle your answer.

42 4 or (40)   86 (6) or 60   51 5 or (50)

71 (1) or 10   37 3 or (30)   62 (2) or 20

96 9 or (90)   14 1 or (10)   79 7 or (70)

83 8 or (80)   25 (5) or 50   43 (3) or 30

Day 160

Tens and Ones

A. Separate tens and ones to complete each addition sentence.

12 = 10 + 2   17 = 10 + 7

24 = 20 + 4   29 = 20 + 9

37 = 30 + 7   46 = 40 + 6

53 = 50 + 3   61 = 60 + 1

B. Combine tens and ones to complete each addition sentence.

20 + 4 = 24   40 + 6 = 46

80 + 7 = 87   30 + 2 = 32

60 + 5 = 65   50 + 1 = 51

70 + 3 = 73

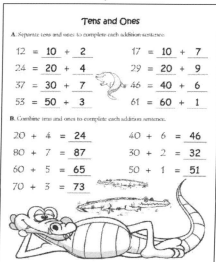

Day 161

Adding and Subtracting Tens

A. Count the number of blocks. Fill in the blanks.

20 + 30 = 50   40 + 30 = 70

60 - 10 = 50   50 - 20 = 30

B. Solve the addition and subtraction problems using tens.

3 tens + 4 tens = 7 tens ⇒ 30 + 40 = 70

2 tens + 6 tens = 8 tens ⇒ 20 + 60 = 80

9 tens - 3 tens = 6 tens ⇒ 90 - 30 = 60

8 tens - 5 tens = 3 tens ⇒ 80 - 50 = 30

Day 162

Adding and Subtracting Tens

Solve the addition and subtraction problems.

3 tens 30	40	20	40	50
+ 5 tens + 50	+ 20	+ 30	+ 40	+ 20
8 tens 80	60	50	80	70

3 tens 30	40	30	20	30
+ 4 tens + 40	+ 50	+ 30	+ 60	+ 20
7 tens 70	90	60	80	50

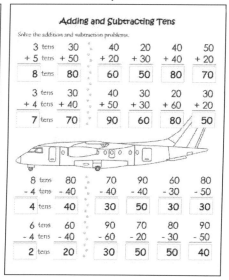

8 tens 80	70	90	60	80
- 4 tens - 40	- 40	- 40	- 30	- 50
4 tens 40	30	50	30	30

6 tens 60	90	70	80	90
- 4 tens - 40	- 60	- 20	- 30	- 50
2 tens 20	30	50	50	40

Day 163

Adding and Subtracting Tens

Solve the addition and subtraction problems.

6 tens 60	20	40	10	20
+ 2 tens + 20	+ 70	+ 30	+ 40	+ 20
8 tens 80	90	70	50	40

2 tens 20	30	20	40	40
+ 3 tens + 30	+ 60	+ 50	+ 50	+ 20
5 tens 50	90	70	90	60

7 tens 70	50	90	70	80
- 5 tens - 50	- 40	- 30	- 30	- 20
2 tens 20	10	60	40	60

6 tens 60	90	70	80	90
- 3 tens - 30	- 20	- 40	- 50	- 80
3 tens 30	70	30	30	10

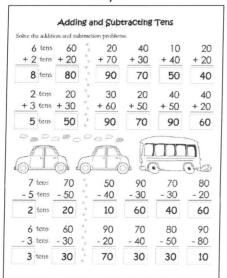

Day 164

Adding and Subtracting Tens

Solve the addition and subtraction problems.

60	20	40	50	30	50
+ 20	+ 30	+ 40	+ 20	+ 60	+ 30
80	50	80	70	90	80

70	20	40	20	30	40
+ 20	+ 20	+ 50	+ 40	+ 30	+ 30
90	40	90	60	60	70

90	70	80	50	70	80
- 70	- 40	- 50	- 30	- 20	- 60
20	30	30	20	50	20

80	90	60	50	90	60
- 40	- 30	- 40	- 20	- 50	- 30
40	60	20	30	40	30

Day 165

Adding and Subtracting Tens

Solve the addition and subtraction problems.

20	30	50	40	20	30
+ 70	+ 30	+ 40	+ 20	+ 20	+ 40
90	60	90	60	40	70

40	50	20	30	60	50
+ 40	+ 20	+ 60	+ 50	+ 30	+ 50
80	70	80	80	90	100

90	70	80	50	70	80
- 20	- 30	- 30	- 20	- 50	- 20
70	40	50	30	20	60

80	90	60	50	90	60
- 40	- 40	- 20	- 30	- 30	- 30
40	50	40	20	60	30